NOTES ON THE
HARVARD TERCENTENARY

The President and Fellows of Harvard College

TO

$\mathcal{G}$REETING:

It having pleased GOD to inspire the love of Learning amongst the first settlers of the Colony of Massachusetts Bay and, in the infancy of their community, to direct their labors towards the well-being of Church and State through the establishment of foundations for the increase of knowledge and the education of youth, it is meet and proper that this Society of Scholars, founded in the Year of Our Lord one thousand six hundred and thirty-six, by Act of a Great and General Court of the Company of Massachusetts Bay convened in Boston the 8th/18th of September of that year, should celebrate in the company of friends and benefactors the THREE HUNDREDTH ANNIVERSARY of its foundation.

FACSIMILE OF THE FIRST PAGE OF THE OFFICIAL INVITATION TO
UNIVERSITIES, COLLEGES, AND LEARNED SOCIETIES

NOTES ON THE

Harvard Tercentenary

*Not that the story need be long, but it
will take a long while to make it short.*

— THOREAU

HARVARD UNIVERSITY PRESS

Cambridge, Massachusetts

1936

PRINTED AT THE HARVARD UNIVERSITY PRESS
CAMBRIDGE, MASSACHUSETTS, U.S.A.

I went to the College Jubilee on the 8th instant. A noble and well-thought-of anniversary. . . . Cambridge at any time is full of ghosts; but on that day the anointed eye saw the crowd of spirits that mingled with the procession in the vacant spaces, year by year, as the classes proceeded; and then the far longer train of ghosts that followed the company, of the men that wore before us the college honors and the laurels of the State — the long, winding train reaching back into eternity.

— EMERSON: *Journals*, September 13, 1836

FOREWORD

THIS brief volume of notes on the Harvard Tercentenary, including the poems and a few of the
speeches which were read or delivered during the
three Tercentenary Days of September 16, 17, and
18, makes no pretense at being a full or definitive
chronicle. Such a volume is now being prepared by
Jerome D. Greene, '96, Director of the Tercentenary
Celebration, to be published some time in 1937. The
sponsors of the present book, written and edited by
David T. W. McCord, '21, have aimed rather at providing a short, readable record of the chief events of
a great occasion. No attempt has been made to in-
clude the detailed reports, programmes, lists of officials and recipients of degrees, which belong — with
the complete text of all speeches — in the official
Tercentenary history. On the other hand, it is hoped
that the chapters which follow will serve their purpose in recalling readily to mind certain now historic
events which must ever be the rightful heritage of all
Harvard men.

THE ASSOCIATED HARVARD CLUBS
Elliott C. Cutler, '09, *President 1935–36*
Mackey Wells, '08, *President 1936–37*

THE HARVARD ALUMNI ASSOCIATION
Learned Hand, '93, *President 1935–36*
F. W. Taussig, '79, *President 1936–37*

THE HARVARD FUND COUNCIL
Lawrence Coolidge, '27, *Chairman 1935–37*

December, 1936.

NOTES ON THE
HARVARD TERCENTENARY

NOTES ON THE HARVARD
TERCENTENARY

I

THE first light fall of Cambridge snow is on the ground as these pages are being prepared for the press. Our private New England autumn which Harvard enjoys in fortunate seclusion from the noise and trample of a part-industrial city is virtually over: leaves raked and gathered in ballooning canvas and carried we know not where; the winter guards of pine and burlap in windless position over perishable shrubs; the last of ivy leaf burned red and ruined on so many ancient walls; the smoke of student fires rising thinly from old brick chimneys; a clear cut of November blue to the deepening sky; a jug of cider sighted on an isolated window ledge; elm and oak and bush gone bare; sparrows and starlings in forage at the south side of Grays and Widener; the cawing of temporary crows; and the long eternal business of life and learning steadied to the pulse of youthful blood.

The visitor in the Yard this morning is aware of this pulse and of the normal activity of an academic day. It might be any of a long succession of Harvard days. If he visited the Yard twelve months ago he will note but little change and no more than two new landmarks — both ancestrally old. He will see the College Pump [1] restored to its original site over the old well in front of Hollis (with a modern bubbler in the interest of sanitation); and the great marble Dragon, presented to Harvard by Alumni in China in honor of her Tercentenary, solemn and perpendicular under the shadow of the Library, wearing for the first time a strange mantle of occidental snow. But our visitor may not be properly aware of one thing of which the Dragon, even more than the pump, persistently reminds us: This is the first snow of the fourth hundred years of Harvard; and this leave-taking of autumn so usual, deliberate, and New England in character is the end of a season of University celebration and "a truly great occasion," as the London *Times* expressed it, unparalleled in the history of our country.

For the passage of two months and the structural clearing of the Yard, much as the autumn winds have cleared her trees, have stripped us clean of all but personal memory of what took place; and it is easier now in retrospect to consider a summer of intense Tercentenary activity and the proceedings of the middle days of September with detached though still fervent delight. The great Tercentenary Theatre whose platform sprang from the steps of the College Church and whose tentative limits were marked by Sever, Widener, and University is gone. The trappings, poles, flags, gonfalons, greens, guidons, seals, crests, lions, and such wonderful paraphernalia, are relics of the

[1] Dedication exercises for the restored College Pump (heavy oak on flagstones) were held on the morning of June 16. Henry Munroe Rogers, '62, Senior Alumnus of the College, accepted the first drink with the remark that water had been a great thing for humanity.

GIFT OF THE CHINESE ALUMNI OF HARVARD

past. The last sound through the marvelous mechanics of electrical broadcast is stilled: speaker, orator, odist, poet, chorus, and symphony. The tide of color: gown, hood, cap, fez, turban, mortar board, brocade, braid, silk, velvet, ermine, tasseled gold, all foreign air and grace, all brilliant to the eye, has faded out. Delegates, dignitaries, ambassadors, friends, and strangers who came to do us honor in being honored; spectator, sharer, alumnus, sons; the ten thousand legendary men of Harvard — they have come and departed. The camera lens is dark. The wires which carried our celebration to the ends of the civilized earth are disconnected. Doer and reporter alike have finished their parts. The gates within gates which stood so white and flawless are cleared and themselves removed. The show is over. Reverence, humility, honor, truth, friendship: these remain. As the Sutra of the Lotus of the Good Law in the country of our Dragon has it, the god of the Tercentenary is now "perfectly extinct upon his throne."

II

The Celebration of the Three Hundredth Anniversary of the Founding of Harvard College was a long celebration which commenced officially on Friday, November 8, 1935, with the exercises held in Sanders Theatre in honor of John Harvard's birthday, and ended with a brilliant three-day climax on September 16, 17, and 18, 1936. Preparations were begun as far back as 1924 when Samuel E. Morison, '08, Professor of History, was appointed Tercentenary Historian.[1] In 1930 the Governing Boards of the University jointly appointed the first Tercentenary Committee, later associated with a committee of the Alumni. This representative group made its principal report to the Corporation in April, 1934; and on May 14, 1934, Jerome D. Greene, '96, was appointed Secretary to the Corporation and Director of the Tercentenary Celebration. His labors to this end, and those of his associates, were long, tireless, scrupulous in detail, and rewarding beyond all expectation.

> I like the scenery
> of the Tercen*teen*ary,
> and behind the scene
> I like Jerome Greene.[2]

[1] His volumes of Harvard History to date (all published by the Harvard University Press) are: "The Founding of Harvard College" (1935); "Harvard College in the Seventeenth Century," 2 vols. (1936); "Three Centuries of Harvard" (1936); "The Development of Harvard University, 1869–1929" (Editor; 1930).

[2] From the present editor's verses in the Tercentenary Graduates' issue of *The Lampoon*.

Though perhaps it did not occur to him, it must have seemed to his associates and to those on the inside that he worked solely under the aegis of the sundial back of Holden Chapel: "On this moment hangs eternity."

By the spring of 1936 all plans were well on the way to completion, and the advent of summer found Cambridge busy with Graduate School sessions and conferences on such diverse matters as soil mechanics, business, education, and theology. From June 15 till September 25, Harvard held open house, described in attractive posters as "Harvard on View." *Salvete omnes!* A marquee was set up in the Straus Hall Quadrangle where pamphlets, folders, catalogues, Tercentenary history, medals, postcards, photographs, and similar Harvardiana were on sale, and where a free guide service maintained its humid headquarters. A second tent was established also in front of the University Museum; and information desks installed at the entrance to Eliot House and in the cloister of Memorial Hall. Over paths and bypaths marked with white black-letter signs bearing the Harvard arms in red, and under a corps of intelligent and fully informed student guides (red coats and megaphones), in fourteen weeks 66,783 recorded visitors from all parts of our country and beyond the seven seas were enabled to tour the grounds and buildings of the University and to see a multitude of rare and important exhibits [1] in the libraries, laboratories,

[1] In addition: The priceless Tercentenary Loan Exhibition of Japanese Art at the Boston Museum of Fine Arts (Sept.–Oct.) including "National

museums, observatories, and classrooms of the College and the Graduate Schools, and of Radcliffe. Caleb Cheeshahteaumuck, that recently revived Indian of engaging name, the first of his race to receive (in 1665) a degree from John Harvard's wilderness College, would have fled in terror before the hourly squads of visitors tramping their way about his sacred wood. Indeed, the drone of megaphonic talk seemed never to stop. Cambridge was like a foreign city: Teachers, parents, children, sightseers, old ladies, old gentlemen, tourists, students, professors with horn-rimmed glasses, Nordics in shorts and binoculars, English in tweeds, Latins in berets and slacks, and Blaschka glass flower veterans listened eagerly for the first time to old legends of a new world . . . "and on your left is Wadsworth House, erected in 1726, the second oldest building in the Yard and the home of nine Harvard presidents." . . . One day a young man, more serious and attentive than his companions, walked with a group, turned his head with their heads, his eyes with their eyes, and absorbed with evident satisfaction the fluent exposition of his student-informer. Yes — and the papers made something of the story — he was James Bryant Conant.

During all these weeks an unprecedented and generously sympathetic press kept Harvard in the national headlines and informed the country at large of

---

Treasures" from the Imperial Household, the Imperial Museum, the Tokyo Art School, and from the private collection of Prince Takamatsu, and many others.

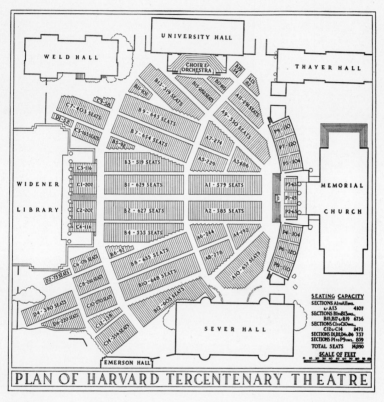

WELD HALL

UNIVERSITY HALL

CHOIR & ORCHESTRA

THAYER HALL

C7 - 403 SEATS

C5 - 165 SEATS

B11 - 101

B13 - 319 SEATS

B15 - 296 SEATS

A11 - 301 SEATS

A9 - 530 SEATS

B9 - 643 SEATS

B7 - 654 SEATS

A7 - 274

C3 - 116

WIDENER

LIBRARY

C1 - 207

C2 - 207

C4 - 116

B3 - 519 SEATS

B5 - 92

A5 - 229

A3 - 486

B1 - 629 SEATS

A1 - 579 SEATS

P3 - 63

P1 - 45

P2 - 63

MEMORIAL

CHURCH

B2 - 627 SEATS

A2 - 585 SEATS

B4 - 535 SEATS

A6 - 244

A4 - 492

B6 - 92

A8 - 278

C6 - 196 SEATS

B8 - 635 SEATS

A0 - 637 SEATS

C8 - 241 SEATS

D2 - 75 SEATS

B10 - 648 SEATS

C10 - 270 SEATS

D4 - 190 SEATS

C12 - 138

B12 - 305 SEATS

D6 - 220 SEATS

C14 - 356 SEATS

SEVER HALL

SEATING CAPACITY
SECTIONS A1 to A11 incl.
to A13   4107
SECTIONS B1 to B13 incl.
B15,B17 to B19   6736
SECTIONS C1 to C10 incl.
C12 to C14   2471
SECTIONS D1,D2,D4, to D6 737
SECTIONS P1 to P9 incl. 839
TOTAL SEATS   14,890

SCALE OF FEET

EMERSON HALL

PLAN OF HARVARD TERCENTENARY THEATRE

WHERE ... "THEY SETTLED LIKE A FLOCK OF IRIDESCENT BIRDS"

meetings and symposia wherein historical truth, scientific discovery, mathematical deduction, cosmic theory, medical research, sociological and economic revolution, and the gracious humanities appeared at the breakfast table as vital and important as the citizen's daily dose of crime and disappointment. For the inner circle, a University publication called *The Tercentenary Gazette*, an old-fashioned illustrated broadside, dedicated to "help alumni and friends of Harvard to enjoy their time in Cambridge during September or any of the intervening months," was issued every fortnight.[1] Under an anonymous editorship it delved into amiable recesses of Harvard history and tradition, and provided the alumnus with a full and detailed calendar of forthcoming Tercentenary events. More officially, every Harvard man had received in the autumn of 1935 a letter from President Conant; and in the spring of 1936 this was followed by a formal University invitation to attend the major ceremonies in September. The distribution of tickets, arrangement for accommodations, and all such administrative matters followed a rigorous schedule. If any Harvard man remained uninformed or uninvited, it was because he had moved to a point on our planet beyond the last lines of communication. At least 10,000 of his fellow alumni were expected back in Cambridge; and the Director's figures show that the estimate was not far wrong: about 10,000 Harvard men, or more than 15,000 people in all, attended the concluding exercises in September. One of them

---

[1] June 12–Sept. 11, 1936.

was Peter Harvard of England, only son of Lionel de Jersey Harvard, '15, and a collateral descendant of the Founder.

Invitations to all Universities, Colleges, and Learned Societies throughout the world, expressing the hope that they would send official delegates to the Tercentenary, were mailed from Cambridge many months in advance of September. The form and wording of these invitations are reproduced on another page. Of the many exhibitions in the University only recently concluded, none was more interesting from the point of view of art, expression, and exquisite taste than that of the hundreds of superbly lettered, printed, illuminated, and inscribed greetings [1] from Harvard's world-wide sister institutions. Many of them startling in perfection and simplicity, they rep-

---

[1] In addition to the formal greetings from Universities, Colleges, Learned Societies, and Institutions, certain others are significant as spontaneous expressions of felicitation; one such being an elaborately illuminated vellum from the Mayor, Aldermen, and Councillors of the Metropolitan Borough of Southwark, John Harvard's birthplace. "It is a matter of considerable pride to us that John Harvard was a native of our Borough. We are gratified by the interest which the governing body of the University has from time to time evinced in the Borough of Southwark. We express the confident hope that the University will further develop the ideals of its Puritan founders and that thereby the world will be assisted in its development of peace, justice, and honor." A second is from sixty-six of the more than 1,200 Cuban school-teachers who attended the Cuban summer school at Harvard in 1900. The greeting concludes: "Help in war, help in peace, help in honorable living among the nations of the earth, that is a summary of what Cuba owes to Harvard University; and therefore we modest and sincere living witnesses of contemporary history hereby certify and proclaim the paramount importance of Harvard's services to our people and the correspondently profound gratitude of ours to this glorious living monument to the ideals of the Pilgrim Fathers."

resent a distinguished addition to the archives of the College Library.

The summer passed: actively, excitedly, expectantly. Toward the end of it the Yard, which used to witness annually the brief assembling of fountains and band stands for Commencement, and still knows the temporary Commencement staging in the Sever Quadrangle, became suddenly alive with building operations. The scaffolding of the Tercentenary Theatre, the grand stand for the chorus, strong aerial bomas in the elms for sound and camera men, gates and flag poles, pedestals and ornaments, flags and bunting, 15,000 collapsible chairs stretching from the College Church (site of old Appleton Chapel) to Widener and past on either flank: carpentry, painting, decoration, and mechanics enough for a fair set in Hollywood; enormous detail, endless minute problems and difficulties — all this represents a story in itself. Not only was the Theatre wired with electrical equipment for amplification, recording, and communication, which the New York *Herald-Tribune* called "the most elaborate ever attempted in the United States," but Sanders Theatre had also to be wired in anticipation of rain, and amplifiers installed in neighboring buildings of auditorium description to accommodate a rainy day crowd. Few people at the exercises could possibly realize the extent of these preparations. Nor did they perhaps consider that without the aid of science such a pageant of the spoken word could not have been held at all. In the final days of tinkering and last adjustment, many

visitors to the still open Yard sat on the fringe of its
15,000 seats in the elm shade and listened to flawless
reproduction of music or the fantastic impromptu
conversations of workmen testing with private utter-
ance the distributed electric tongues.[1]

It was hot, brown, Cambridge-like post-summer
weather. The days slipped on toward the fall; and
one day at the end of August seventy-two scholars
from all over the United States and from many
foreign countries arrived for the Tercentenary Conference of Arts and Sciences held in the College
buildings from August 31 to September 12. Sixty-
two of this number were to receive honorary degrees
from Harvard at the exercises on September 18; the
other ten, Harvard had previously honored. These
conferences in the four quadrants of learning (Humanities; Physical, Biological, and Social Sciences)
were in general open to small groups of spectators, in
addition to professors, teachers, and specialists in each
field; but there were also public lectures by world-
renowned authorities, including many winners of the
Nobel Prize: Eddington, Svedberg, Fischer, Jung,
Hopkins, Spemann, Krogh, Maunier, Bergius, and
others; and the sessions provided in various languages
such symposia as: "Authority and the Individual,"
"Factors Determining Human Behavior;" and such
lectures as "Mediaeva Universalism and its Present
Value," "Stability and Social Change," "Hellenism

---

[1] In one of these highly audible official tests, before an audience of
astonished transients and arrested squirrels, a second honorary degree
was awarded (with variations) to George Washington (LL.D. 1776).

MEETING IN THE FACULTY ROOM: OPENING PRESIDENT QUINCY'S PACKAGE. DR. DAVID CHEEVER, '97, PRESIDENT CONANT, PROFESSOR R. P. BLAKE, PRESIDENT LOWELL, HENRY C. CLARK, '11

and Christianity." President Conant and Jerome D. Greene, Chairman of the Executive Committee of the Conference, made the opening addresses, and many of the papers [1] read during the two weeks were sent out on the air. The Square, the Yard, and contiguous Cambridge appeared brisk with distinguished visitors whose silver Tercentenary medals and gray, green, yellow, and blue ribbons (according to their quadrant) gleamed in the sunlight. Everyone a little excited . . . the sound of French, Italian, German, Spanish, Japanese . . . ritual of the megaphone boys and the footfalls of their charges . . . the final ceremonies rapidly approached.

On Tuesday, September 8, a *pro forma* meeting of the Harvard Alumni Association was held in the Faculty Room of University Hall in the presence of President Lowell, Professor Samuel E. Morison, Professor R. P. Blake, Director of the University Library, Members of the Governing Boards, Deans, certain Faculty Members, and invited guests. Its immediate purpose was the opening by President Conant of a package sealed by President Josiah Quincy in 1836. Dr. David Cheever, '97, Vice-President of the Association presided. Under a barrage of floodlights and motion picture cameras, the package was unsealed, and found to contain (as Mr. Conant has said) "letters from the Alumni of Harvard College and, unfortunately, nothing else." The Meeting was thereupon adjourned until Friday, September 18,

---

[1] To be published in 1937, in three vols., by the Harvard University Press.

1936. . . . On Sunday, September 13, at 8 P.M., Professor A. T. Davison, o6, and guest organists gave an organ recital in the Memorial Church. . . . On Monday and Tuesday, September 14 and 15, the Tercentenary Session of the Medical School held symposia in Boston in the mornings and afternoons. . . . In Sanders Theatre at 4 P.M. on the same afternoons the Boston String Quartet gave two of a series of three remarkable chamber concerts whose programmes were devoted entirely to the compositions of Harvard Graduates.[1] . . . The next three days will be known to Harvard history as The Tercentenary Days.

[1] Arthur Foote, '74; Frederick S. Converse, '93; Edward Burlingame Hill, '94; Daniel Gregory Mason, '95; John Alden Carpenter, '97; William C. Heilman, 'oo; Edward Ballantine, '07; Randall Thompson, '20; Walter Piston, '24.

III

September 16 was a fair, inviting day. The third
and last of the chamber concerts was given and received enthusiastically in Sanders Theatre at 11 A.M.
At a two o'clock private ceremony in the Widener
Library, Alexander Dunlop Lindsay, Vice-Chancellor
of Oxford University, presented to President Conant,
as Oxford's Tercentenary gift to Harvard, a letter [1]
by Christopher Columbus concerning "the newly
discovered islands," and printed in book form in 1493.
This gift out of the great Bodleian Library is one of
the only two copies of the first edition known to
exist.... That afternoon the Undergraduate Delegates
from other Universities and Colleges were enter-
tained by Harvard undergraduates in Eliot House
Court. In the evening there was a dinner to the
Council of the Associated Harvard Clubs at the
Harvard Club of Boston; and at 9 P.M. in Symphony
Hall the first of the three Tercentenary Concerts by
Serge Koussevitzky, LL.D. (Hon.) '29, and the Boston Symphony Orchestra.

But the brilliant event of the day was the reception
of Delegates from other Universities, Colleges, and
Learned Societies, held in Sanders Theatre at three
in the afternoon. To these Delegates the Harvard
circle and the friends of Harvard living in Cambridge, Boston, and Greater Boston had opened their
doors in generous hospitality and welcomed them as
their guests. To their entertainment every possible

[1] *Epistola de Insulis Noviter Repertis.*

thought was given, including many private dinners in their honor. The number of Delegates at the reception was 547, and they represented 530 Universities, Colleges, and Learned Societies, and came from forty-six states in the Union, two Territories, and forty foreign countries. Of this number many, of course, were included in the group of seventy-two scholars who had previously participated in the Tercentenary Conference of Arts and Sciences.

The time drew on to three o'clock. The silver medals and ribbons became now but the smallest accents of color in the undulate sea of gowns, hoods, caps, of all hues and fashions, as Dignitaries, Delegates, Fellows, Faculty Members, Presiding Officers, College and University Presidents, and guests of both sexes assembled in Sanders. *Salvete omnes!* No detail of the ceremonial days was more carefully executed than the official reception of these 547 men who had come to do Harvard honor on her three-hundredth birthday. The presentation was ordered by the ranking age of the Institution represented. If there was more than one Delegate, the Institution was asked to rank them according to its own standard of seniority. The Delegates were accordingly formed in prearranged columns in Memorial Hall. After President Conant, Jerome D. Greene, as Director of the Tercentenary, President Lowell, and all guests had been seated, leaving the floor seats of Sanders Theatre empty, Dr. Reginald Fitz, '06, University Marshal, announced the name of each College, University, and Learned Society, and its Dele-

HERE GATHERED "THOUSANDS IN HIS HONOR AND HIS PRAISE:" PART OF THE THEATRE IN THE YARD, LOOKING TOWARD THE MEMORIAL CHURCH AND THE TERCENTENARY STAGE

gate (or Delegates in turn) stepped forward from a line entering at the north of the platform and was formally presented to President Conant, who shook his hand. The first Delegate to come forward was Professor Saleh Hashem Attia from Al-Azhar University in Cairo, which was founded in 970, or 666 years before the founding of Harvard.[1]

Past the marble standing figures of Josiah Quincy and James Otis, the learned men of Paris, Oxford, Cambridge, St. Andrews, Rome, Peking, Brussels, Buenos Aires, Tokyo, Havana, Copenhagen, Munich, Rangoon, Beirut, Oslo, Cracow, Madrid, Leiden, Istanbul, Cape Town, and scores beside, descended in rustling silk and chromatic harmony to their places. "As brilliant as the rainbow and as dignified as the Supreme Court," said the Boston *Herald* in its account. But there was another harmony perceived in the printed programme; and this lay in the reverential recital of Saxon and foreign names which could be made to run like a sentence in Sir Thomas Browne:[2] "The Very Rev. Mgr. Francesco Lardone, Prof. Sir Sarvepalli Radhakrishnan, Prof. Jack Henry Sandground."

President Conant made the address of welcome; and Professor Elie Cartan, Delegate of the University of Paris, one of the "great Universities from which we are proud to claim our descent," made response for all Delegates present.

[1] Delegate of the youngest University was Dr. Octavio Méndez Pereira of the Universidad de Panamá, founded in 1935.

[2] *E.g.*: "According to the ordainer of order and mystical mathematicks of the City of Heaven."

"On behalf of the Governing Boards and Faculties of Harvard University," said President Conant, "I bid you welcome. . . . As the President of the most ancient [of American foundations for higher education in the United States], I may claim the privilege of addressing a special salutation this afternoon to those who come from foreign lands. Gentlemen from afar, we receive you gladly not only as Delegates to Harvard's Tercentenary Celebration but as ambassadors accredited to all the universities and colleges of this republic. . . . Ladies and gentlemen, the greetings which you bring to Harvard we thankfully accept. In these messages of good will we read the continued aspiration of mankind toward a universal fellowship based on human reason . . . a fellowship which transcends all barriers of race and nation. . . ."

Professor Cartan, pontifically splendid amid splendor, made his response in French: a response delightful for its grace, sincerity, and singleness of phrase. Of Harvard Alumni he said (in English equivalent): "Here they learned the primacy of spiritual values. . . . If the world, emerging from the trouble and anxiety of the present hour, may at some future time find a spiritual unity more universal and more stable than that which Christendom enjoyed in the Middle Ages, it pleases us to think that Harvard University . . . will have helped us in the search for this unity."

But it is the burst of color in the Delta, whence the dismissed assembly proceeded to tea, that remains in the memory of the spectator as the most magnificent and poetic interlude of all. It was one of those beautiful wine-like middle September afternoons such as New Englanders rightly claim can occur only in New England. The sky, sun, wind, and air were all of one temper to the occasion. Out of Memorial Hall streamed the bright gowns: blue and purple mingling with subtle shades of Oxford, Cambridge, and Sorbonne red; with the dark kimono of Japan, the green and gold braid of the various Academies of the Institut de France; with the fur-edged gown and chain-of-office of the Mayor of the Borough of Southwark, and the uniforms of the service; with what hundred other gowns and hoods showing scarlet, yellow, orange, lilac; with uniforms, medals, swords, pacific and military caps; with plumes and pompons, ermine and velvet; with shades and values as on some great palette: marvelous and romantic as when Stevenson said "but the Camisards had only bright and supporting visions!" Bright and supporting visions of faces, persons, minds; of distinction, cultivation, and individuality. A man wandered about in a kind of mental and rainbow aberration. Many will remember that sight: men and women of all races talking lightly in the fellowship of a common and magnificent interest; brought together in one place in one country over one historical occurrence which perhaps at some time had touched the lives of each of them. Or some will remember it personified in the serenely single figure of Professor Alfred North Whitehead,[1] wrapped in a scarlet Cambridge gown; caught for a moment as solitary as scholarship, yet radiant as a lived philosophy.

[1] His retirement as of September 1, 1937, has just been announced.

IV

On Thursday, September 17, under leaden and vainly threatening clouds, the emphasis changed sharply from scholar to alumnus. The morning opened at 9.30 with a Service of Thanksgiving and Remembrance in The Memorial Church. The audience which came by invitation included members of the Governing Boards, the several Faculties, distinguished guests of the University, representatives of all alumni bodies and of every living College Class, and a delegation of undergraduates. They were deeply rewarded by fine music and a memorable service distinguished for this hauntingly beautiful prayer offered by The Reverend Charles Edwards Park, S.T.D. (Hon.) '32:

"Almighty God, the God of our fathers, all our blessings come from thee. Without thee there can be nothing strong, and nothing holy. In each high moment of life our thoughts turn to thee; and we ask thee to bless unto us the purpose of this hour.

"We come before thee with offerings of heartfelt gratitude for the guidings of thy Providence in the past; for the temper which was in our forefathers, their reverence and godly fear, their quick sense of accountability to thee, which made them eager instruments of thy Will; their austere righteousness and fearless faith, prompting them to hazard all for conscience, and teaching them that the mind is thy gift, the truth thine handmaid, and that the spirit of wisdom and understanding proceedeth from thee alone.

"We praise thee that in their day of arduous labor a prescience warned them of greater days to come, and instructed them to build a foundation broad and deep. We praise thee that, knowing thy truth to be their only assurance of freedom, and wise to desire more wisdom, they founded this University, to preserve and increase their little treasure of learning, and to guide their rulers in the way of understanding.

"As on this day we glorify thee for its unbroken continuance through the centuries, for its steadfast growth in honor and power and loyalty to thy truth, we call to mind the wise men who have served it in their generations, their fidelity and unselfish devotion, and the endowment they have left unto it of noble character and integrity.

"We call to mind the rich men who have seen its needs and foreseen its possibilities, who have strengthened its hands and multiplied its resources, rejoicing to share with it their prosperity, and finding in its larger service their sufficient reward.

"We call to mind the fathers and mothers of our land whose love and hope and pride have centered upon this place, who have looked unto it with confidence, and have made their unapplauded sacrifices that their sons might enter upon a fairer heritage.

"We call to mind the young men in their multitudes who have felt its touch and learned its spirit, whose innocence has been trained to strength and whose strength has been disciplined by wisdom and self-control, and who have gone forth to welcome the task and problem of life with feet that were swift and souls that were jubilant.

"Eternal God, Searcher of hearts, from whom no thought can be hid, if in any way we have done injury to this University, if we have misunderstood its ideal or misused its gifts, if we have tainted its good name by false pride, or narrowed its high spirit by prejudice and jealousy, or if we have betrayed its confidence by unworthy ambition, we beseech thee to accept our penitence and grant us thy forgiveness.

"Enable us henceforth to see the breadth and brightness of its opportunity as a servant of thy holy Will. Grant us to feel something of the olden-time reverence for right and truth and justice and principle, the olden-time eagerness to learn thy ways and share thy creative labor. Grant that this University, disciplined but unfettered by the past, inspired and undismayed by the future, may go on from strength to strength to guide thy children into thy more abundant life, to be their defense against vanity, passion, and error, and to make them again the Lord's Free People.

"Grant that each one of us may find a personal reconsecration to all that is fair and true and holy, as we rededicate this University to the years of the Right Hand of the Most High.

"And to thee, O God, be the glory, world without end. Amen."

During the early forenoon members of the Associated Harvard Clubs, many of them fresh in New England for the most important meeting of that or-

ganization since the founding in 1897, signed names
and collected badges under a temporary marquee in
the mall in front of the Boston Club. They were out
in Cambridge by ten or ten-thirty, and thereupon
joined the departing congregation from the Church to
find their pick of seats in the great theatre to which
their red tickets admitted them. Gray skies meant
nothing. It could not rain. It was a day of reunion,
of renewal — of revision, even. Many of these men
had not been in Cambridge since they were graduated
before the War, before two wars; before change had
raised so white a spire above the elms, had reared
so huge a library, strung so high a fence, or pushed
the frontiers of the green Yard down to the river. It
was a family day; a day of youth (and not a little
sentiment) returned. It was a day of old associations, "hoping for Kitty or Copey or Bliss." [1] *Salvete*

[1] Laurence McKinney, '12, in the Tercentenary Graduates' issue of
The Lampoon. The subjects, of course, are Professors *emeriti* George
Lyman Kittredge, '82, Charles Townsend Copeland, '82, and Bliss Perry,
Litt.D. (Hon.) '25.

> How many years? Why it's over twenty, —
>   We have seen triumphs and treaties go —
> We have come back through want and plenty
>   Looking for scenes that we used to know —
> Gone from the Yard is the Class Day fountain,
>   The Graduate gropes in a strange abyss
> Seeking a landmark, a reckoning mountain,
>   Hoping for Kitty or Copey or Bliss.
>
> Gone the sarcophagus known as Gore —
>   The Library's longer and Widener now —
> The Appleton Chapel stands no more,
>   The Frog Museum is changed — and how!
> Houses have bloomed on the river's brim —
>   But what in the name of Conant is this? —

omnes! The long gonfalons of red and yellow filled in the occasional breeze; heraldic devices [1] of Lowell, Dunster, Winthrop, Kirkland, Eliot; of Law, Divinity, and Medicine, delighted the modern crusader's eye. The gold lions of John Harvard's Emmanuel stood upright on their white poles. The seats filled rapidly. On the camouflaged platforms erected in the trees — camera, wire, and sound stood ready. The golden weather vane on the Church shifted uneasily. Notables, Dignitaries, Delegates, Officials in morning dress, found their places on the stage. People on the fringe kept drifting in. As amazing as anything else, one thought: that this great sea of life and color walled in to itself could become so utterly remote from the rest of the Yard of which it was now the heart.

> Clear from a far and glowing break of day,
> Harvard, you speak. . . .
> Once more, the wilderness?   And a new world?

Eleven o'clock: a simmering quiet . . . the crown-

> And what is *that* architectural whim?
> We'll have to ask Kitty or Copey or Bliss.
>
> .   .   .   .   .   .
>
> Baker is gone to a heavenly setting —
> And Neilson fled to a flock of femmes,
> The ghost of Wendell we know is getting
> A gorging of hot conversational gems.
> The crinkled smile on the Dean's kind face is
> Gone with a myriad smiles we miss;
> So please, dear God, don't fill the places
> Quite yet of Kitty and Copey and Bliss.

[1] These and other ornaments after the design of Pierre la Rose, '95, were part of the decorative setting designed by the late Charles A. Coolidge, '81, and his partner, Henry R. Shepley, '10, architects of the Tercentenary Theatre.

Greetings:

The Harvard Club of Kansas City
sends greetings from the
Heart - of - America.

All the Harvard men in our territory join in celebrating the three hundredth anniversary of Harvard. When we consider the glorious achievements of the University, we are proud to be numbered in the society of men who have studied within her walls. We are proud to know that Harvard has grown to be one of the greatest seats of learning in the entire world and we look forward to the future believing that the name of Harvard will be engraved even deeper in the minds of scholars as the great outpost in the exploration of the unknown and a great teacher of all the branches of Knowledge.

A PAGE FROM ONE OF THE MANY GREETINGS OF THE
ASSOCIATED HARVARD CLUBS

and-pennant weather vane shifted again. . . . Three hundred years! The Reverend Minot Simons, '91, ascended the tribune and pronounced the Invocation. Dr. Elliott C. Cutler, '09, President of the Associated Harvard Clubs, thereupon called the Meeting to order:

"Mr. President and Fellows of Harvard College, Mr. President and Members of the Board of Overseers, Your Excellency the Governor of the Commonwealth, our Host the Harvard Club of Boston, distinguished and honored Guests, Gentlemen of Harvard, Ladies: I now call this gathering to order. Lest there be some doubt as to why I, whose life is spent in hospitals, should preside today, let all recall that a doctor is usually present at birth, and I come to you as a physician to initiate this Tercentenary occasion in its first steps.

"We meet today as part of a great session to honor the Universities of the World, to acclaim the value to humanity of the scholarly and inquisitive mind, to uphold free speech, and in particular to do service again to Harvard University. Nothing created by man has had a more vigorous, useful, and prolonged existence than the universities. They have had their ups and downs; political, social, and religious upheavals have pushed them from their forward course, but always they have returned to assume their certain duty — the grouping together of students and teachers to inquire, to investigate, to study for the benefit of mankind.

"No graduate ever repays in any sense his obligation to the university that assisted his awakening spirit, so that this great gathering can be taken as another gesture of our Alumni expressing their gratitude and devotion to Harvard. That Harvard has grown in size and has assumed a leading role in the destinies of our people should make us very happy, and that these, our distinguished colleagues, have gathered from the ends of the earth to assist us on this occasion should emphasize to each and every graduate both his good fortune in being an element of Harvard, and his desire to be of greater service to the Harvard of the future.

"The Associated Harvard Clubs was formed by an ardent band of Harvard graduates in 1897 in the middle western states. The spirit of the pioneer has helped its personnel to a deep devotion to Harvard. As President of the Associated Harvard Clubs for this year I preside today, and now have the pleasure of calling upon our Regional Vice-Presidents for a report of the greetings they bring to Harvard from the clubs within their district. Will the delegates of the respective clubs please rise and stand during the presentation of their greetings by their Vice-President."

The delegates of the respective clubs each rose in turn as the Regional Vice-Presidents [1] presented greetings to Harvard amid much applause.

---

[1] New England: Thorvald S. Ross, '12; Eastern, H. V. Blaxter, '05; South Central, Ralph H. Hallett, '04; Southern, Harold Bush-Brown, '11; Central, W. O. Batchelder, '05; West Central, Philip Little, Jr., '09;

Dr. Cutler then introduced President Conant, and the audience rose in spontaneous applause. For many it was the first intimate glimpse of this graduate of the Class of 1914, the internationally known young chemist who had succeeded President Lowell in 1933, becoming the twenty-third holder of Harvard's highest office. Mr. Conant ascended the tribune almost as if aware of this. The crowd fell doubly silent. He began to speak clearly and without effort, his voice and sharp enunciation carrying, as through previous and impending speeches, to the outer edges of the crowd. He welcomed the Associated Harvard Clubs to Cambridge: "The future of this republic will be affected in no small measure by what you think and by what you believe. . . . At this time of our celebration Harvard men might well look backwards not only at Harvard's history but at three centuries of human activity. . . . If we can learn anything from such history it is surely that in the past patience and courage have won victories for the life of the spirit. Can we believe that in the future it will be otherwise?" This in extract; but the full conclusion of

---

Southwest Central and Southwestern, Fermor Spencer Church, '21; North and South Pacific and the Orient, Rudolph Altrocchi, '08; Canadian, Herbert L. Sanborn, '08; European, F. Herman Gade, '92. The collected greetings filled fifty-six typescript pages, and their tenor of devotion and homage is reflected in this sentence from the Harvard Club of Western Pennsylvania: "Your spirit is ever conscious of the amazement of the questioning stars, the ceaseless challenge of events, the inexhaustible appetite for adventure; and as your faith, your confidence, and your hope are ever strong and enduring, you will always wear the crown of immortality."

President Conant's remarks is important here for two episodes of sentiment on which it turns:

"And now I shall seal a package which will be placed in the Harvard archives to be opened in the fall of 2036. This package contains letters from some of the officials of the University addressed to their successors a hundred years later and certain material collected by the Director of the Tercentenary Celebration."

The package was then handed to President Conant by David M. Little, '18; and with proper ceremony and some adhesion difficulty this was sealed by him, to be opened by the President of Harvard University in 2036 (and not before). Mr. Conant continued:

"As you all know, President Quincy sealed a package of letters a hundred years ago and wrote on the outside of the package in his own hand the following inscription:

Letters from Alumni of Harvard College written in August 1836; responding to the invitation of the Committee of Arrangements for the Centennial [sic] Celebration commemorative of the foundation of that institution.

To be opened by the President of Harvard College in the year 1936 and not before.

Pursuant to Josiah Quincy's directions, I had the privilege of opening this package at the small meeting of the Alumni Association held in the Faculty Room of University Hall on September 8 this year. An inspection of the contents showed that the package contained, indeed, letters from the Alumni of Harvard College and, unfortunately, nothing else.

The letters from the Alumni have been examined by our official historian, Professor Morison, and he will publish a report in a few days. I have been permitted by him to quote from certain sections of his summary. In the first place, Professor Morison points out that although the package may have been closed in 1836 it could not have been sealed until 1844, as the seal used was the one adopted by the Corporation on December 30, 1843. This seal was the first actual die ever cut with *Veritas* on the books. I have just used this same, identical seal in closing the package which is to be opened one hundred years hence. Mr. Morison reports that in the package sealed by Quincy there were 436 letters from the Alumni of which about sixty per cent were acceptances of Mr. Winthrop's invitation to attend the Bicentennial meeting. A number of these letters are of interest because of the autographs,[1] and others are interesting because of the contents. Time permits me to read only a few. One of the most striking and optimistic is that of the Reverend Peter Eaton of the Class of 1787, minister of West Boxford, who wrote as follows of his Alma Mater:

As a literary institution she stands preëminent; but, a combined effort has been made by religious intolerance to crush her. Although this effort has been successful in diminishing her numbers; she still lives and flourishes. I put a persuasion, as knowledge is increased, free inquiry indulged, (in which, she leads in the march,) as truth is

---

[1] Four are those of Francis Parkman, Class of 1807; Edward Everett, 1811; Ralph Waldo Emerson, 1821; and Wendell Phillips, 1831.

more clearly displayed to view, from ye rubbish in which it has been buried, she will assume her former prominence, for "great is the truth and strongest of all things." Its progress is hard, for it has to encounter early education prejudice, ignorance, the pride of party; yet its triumph is, ultimately, certain. That Harvard may live & flourish— the day rendered pleasant to her Sons, is the sincere desire & prayer of your humble servant

P. Eaton

"Samuel Atkins Eliot of the Class of 1817, who was later Treasurer of Harvard College, writes about certain arrangements for the celebration which he had agreed to undertake for President Quincy, and apologizes for his lateness in attending to the matters because of the serious illness of his two-year-old boy. As Professor Morison remarks in his report: 'It was lucky for Harvard that this baby recovered, for his name was Charles William Eliot.'

"It is comforting to know that among the Harvard Alumni of one hundred years ago there were those who wished to enter a protest. It has, apparently, always been a characteristic of Harvard College that among its graduates one can count on an ample number of critics. As a representative of this important branch of the Harvard family one hundred years ago, I may put forward a gentleman from Philadelphia who wrote as follows:

Excuse me for this frank expression of my feelings. I owe nothing to the President, professors and tutors of Harvard College in office from A D 1810 to A D 1814.

"But almost all the replies were in a different vein, and although Harvard individuality is shown by the language (no two replies being alike), the general sentiment is perhaps summed up by Samuel Wragg of the Class of 1790, of Charleston, who concluded his letter with this sentence:

May the Sons of Harvard University celebrate her centenial [*sic*] anniversaries to the end of time, each celebration witnessing her encreasing prosperity and reputation.

With this sentiment which we are glad to echo on this occasion, I conclude my report on the contents of the package sealed by President Quincy.

"In addition to this package [continued the President] there has been reposing in the Harvard archives for one hundred years another object of perhaps even greater interest to this gathering this morning. The last speaker at the alumni meeting on September 8, 1836, began his address with these words: 'The occasion and the place on which we are now assembled connect us with the past and future.' Referring then to the fact that none of his hearers would be present at the Tercentenary Celebration, and that even the memory of a great majority would have perished, he said:

[But] it is a boon [for us] to be permitted to see, even with the eye of the imagination, that promised land which we may not enter. Creatures of a day, it is delightful to multiply our associations with that distant time. In this spirit, the banner that floats over us has been prepared. It will be deposited among the archives of the University. Our hope is, that a century hence it will collect under its folds the Alumni of Harvard. Over what a scene will it on that day display its blazonry! What a feeling of relationship will it establish between that age and the present!

"That banner, Gentlemen, which was deposited indeed in the archives of the University, is now ready to be raised over this gathering of the Alumni of Harvard. Dr. Cutler, will you raise the flag!"

Dr. Cutler issued a brief command. The old flag, gray-white against the dull sky, shook out of its century folds as it was slowly raised by Charles H. Watkins, '09. It hung lifeless in the still air, but its meaning was alive.

"Gentlemen," concluded the President, "the hope of a hundred years ago has been fulfilled."

Threat of rain, but no rain fell. Music — "Ten Thousand Men of Harvard" — followed by three undergraduate addresses: Rendigs Thomas Fels, '39, of Cincinnati, "Freshman Life in the Yard Today;" Norman Lee Cahners, '37, of Bangor, "The Changing Aspect of Harvard Athletics;" Edward Oehler Miller, '37, of St. Louis, "The Undergraduate of Today."   Edward Miller, last of the three to speak, said in part — and in example of the modern undergraduate mind at work:

"Prominent among the changed attitudes of the undergraduate today is a marked increase in social responsibility. The inertia implied in resignation to a system of laissez-faire is being challenged by a scientific search for that form of society most conducive to the common good. The undergraduate's zeal for earning a living is being replaced by a desire to participate intelligently in later civic activities.

"In this increased sense of undergraduate social responsibility, Harvard has shown that she must

THURSDAY MORNING NEAR THE TRIBUNE: "THY SONS TO THY JUBILEE THRONG."

avoid aloofness from the outer world. She has, with fluctuations, been a dominating force in the past in national and international affairs. Today she is trying earnestly to face the new problems which have arisen. We may confidently predict that, in doing so, she will avoid the evil of attempting to teach her future social leaders what to think, instead of how to think. . . .

"Another change in the undergraduate of today is his attitude toward extra-curricular activities. He does not, in general, feel that a crowded social and extra-curricular calendar is necessarily a mark of distinction, or of collegiate success. More and more, he is choosing his extra-curricular activities to supplement his college training as a whole — to suit him better for his later, more practical life. . . . This is a tendency that is becoming more and more pronounced. It indicates the undergraduate's feeling that extra-curricular activities should be treated as a means to a chosen end, rather than as an ultimate end in themselves.

"These are some of the more important consequences of the recent changes in the social and academic life of Harvard College. Other accomplishments, equally important, might be mentioned, but there still remains much to be done. Consider, for example, the House Plan. The Houses, equipped with ample libraries, comfortable common rooms, billiard rooms, squash courts, and music rooms, to say nothing of the dining halls which offer the most valuable means of acquaintance, have been of great value in giving purpose to the undergraduate's scholastic pursuits. He is now made to feel, by his very surroundings, that he is part of a vast intellectual activity, and that even his recreation may be directed toward the common goal. They make him realize his increased social responsibility. But, although the Houses have been a true blessing to undergraduate life, they have fallen short of their goal in several respects. Instead of integrating the College into one great whole, they have tended to break it up into separate units. They have restricted friendships, to a great extent, to members of the same House. Paradoxical as it may seem, the Houses might well serve to integrate the College as a whole, if more individual House spirit were developed. For a developed House spirit would lead to an increase in competition between the Houses — and such wholesome rivalry would tend to bring the diverse parts of the College together. . . .

"A conspicuous characteristic of the past decade is a growing feeling of intimacy on the part of the young generation with their elders. In the College, this has revealed itself in an ever-increasing desire among the students to have more personal acquaintance with the members of the faculty. The Houses, where faculty and students may dine together, have done a good deal toward meeting these demands, but much is still desired by the students. The older members of the faculty, with large courses and heavy administrative duties, as well as with the guidance of graduate students and with their own research work, have too little time for personal contact with the undergraduates. This represents one of a very few instances where the College has not succeeded in adapting itself to the changed spirit of its new generation. Through the increased coöperation of both the faculty and the undergraduate members, the Houses must be utilized to the fullest as educational no less than as social units, for only thus can Harvard College's future be planned and ultimately determined, by the mutual efforts of students and teachers. . . .

"The undergraduate of today is gratified at the great measure of freedom which the college authorities now allow him. The effect of this freedom on the student is his assumption of a large share of the responsibility for his own education. And it is safe to predict that this freedom will be no less when the College celebrates its four-hundredth birthday. Harvard has had a brilliant past. These recent developments show that Harvard, aware of the great changes that are taking place in the society of which she is a part, is prepared, now as always, to furnish that intellectual leadership which has invariably been her glory. . . ."

Looking back to the 250th Celebration, in 1886, we find Dr. Oliver Wendell Holmes looking forward to our own 300th. He is looking, of course, in autocratic verse (of the order of 450 lines):

So when the third ripe century stands complete,
As once again the sons of Harvard meet,
Rejoicing, numerous as the sea-shore sands,
Drawn from all quarters, — farthest distant lands . . .

These tinkling lines, oblivion's easy prey,
Once more emerging to the light of day,
Not all unpleasing to the listening ear
Shall wake the memories of this bygone year. . . .

But further back than such days of "reckless and swaggering prosperity," as James Russell Lowell viewed Dr. Holmes's time, went Hermann Hagedorn, '07, in his Tercentenary Ode: [1]

HARVARD, WHAT OF THE LIGHT?

Light is not light, that lights the mind alone.
Clear from a far and glowing break of day,
Harvard, you speak: "Light is not light, that lights
Only a part, with cold moon-brightness, leaving
The rest to darkness and the whole to the storm.
Light, that is light, is light for the whole man."
Oh, light, complete, creative, shining, kindling!
Flame in the mind, flame in the heart, white flame
Upreaching infinitely to white flames,
Austere, obedient in their ordered gyres:
The light you bore, the light that bore you, Harvard!

Three hundred years, Harvard, three hundred years!
Out of your light, like fiery birds upspringing,
Runners, runners, with torches! The wilderness
    upreared,
Monstrous, with talons raised. The wilderness,
    blinded,
With head averted, withdrew.

[1] Both the Ode and the Phi Beta Kappa Poem were to be given by Robert Frost, '01, who withdrew because of illness.

Out of your light, Harvard,
A fire on the hearth, a lamp on the hill, a crackling
Beacon, proclaiming to darkness, the deathless
Creator of light!

Out of your light,
Brave hearts, large minds! Out of your light, heroic,
Indomitable souls! Forerunners, captains, upholders!
Rebels and sages! Prophets! Breakers of idols!
Delvers in darkness! Watchers by lonely headlands!
Contrivers of magic! Summoners of the invisible!
Kindlers of fires!
Out of your light, Harvard!

Out of your light,
Cities and states! Out of your light, resounding
Bells in high towers! White beams, exploring the
    hidden
Interstices of electrons, the secret
Vagaries of stars!
Out of your light, light! Out of your faith, faith!
Out of your love, the open hand, the outstretched
Encompassing pity. Out of your listening spirit,
A word, a way! Out of your hushed obedience,
Harvard, a new world!

Light is not light that lights not the whole man.
New worlds grow old. Harvard, what of the un-
    fathomed
Oceans, breaking, deep-toned, in successive to-
    morrows?

What of the night, Harvard? What of the lamentation
Under your windows, the moaning of multitudes,
   crying? —
"Light blazes on us, and we shake in darkness.
Light clothes our bodies, and we die of cold."
What of the dearth, Harvard? What of the hunger?
The fear, the fever, the desolation, the icy
Whistling of winds through infinite, arctic spaces,
Dividing man and man?   What of the cleaving,
What of the heaving ground, the bodies hurtling
From towers, towers toppling, the terror, the swirl-
   ing fury,
The trampling feet, the drums rolling?   Youth, in
   vacuity,
Gasping for daybreak!

What of the night, Harvard?
A wilderness uprears, with talons raised!
What of the light, Harvard?
The light you bore, you breathed on, you made live?
Once more, Harvard, ships on a stormy sea?
Once more, Harvard, the foot on the perilous shore?
Once more, runners with torches?   Beacons, pro-
   claiming
Once more, once more, the ineluctable Christ?
Harvard,
Once more, the wilderness?   And a new world?

   With appropriate ceremony, and to "keep alive to
future generations the wit, the love, the holiness, of
his face," a bust of the late Dean Le Baron Russell

Briggs, '75, was unveiled by his grandson, L. B. R. Briggs, 3rd, and presented to the University by Professor Joseph H. Beale, '82, in behalf of a few of the Dean's legion of friends. It has since been placed in the Faculty Room of University Hall.

Presentation to Harvard of the Chinese stone Dragon, gift of the Harvard Alumni in China, was made by Fred C. Sze, '18, President of the Harvard Club of Shanghai. Many of the audience on their way to the southwest theatre gate had paused to observe it in its present location just off the path along the west side of Widener and in front of Boylston Hall.[1] To the occidental eye it appears half tortoise, half dragon, towering twenty feet, supporting on its back (see illustration) a black stone tablet in which is cut in beautiful Chinese characters the appropriate oriental dedication. A monument out of the Ch'ing Dynasty (1796–1821), it was originally presented by the Emperor to a Governor of his provinces. President Sze, in a graceful and moving speech, concluded with a quotation of an ancient Chinese poet:

> Take this not as a fair repayment
> But as a pledge of enduring love.

Dr. Masaharu Anesaki, Delegate of the Imperial Academy of Japan, and one of the sixty-two recipients of honorary degrees on September 18, presented the University with a Japanese stone lantern,[2] un-

---

[1] Boylston Hall now contains the Harvard-Yenching Institute and the Chinese-Japanese Library.

[2] Gift of the Harvard Club of Japan.

veiled in front of the platform. This lantern, "of nearly the same age as Harvard, perhaps a little younger," will probably be placed in the garden of the Fogg Art Museum. It stands about six feet high, and was selected by Baron Ino Dan of Tokyo, a Harvard graduate student, '18–'19. To the Japanese a lantern "symbolizes light, the light that dispels the darkness of illusion, and it is dedicated everywhere in Japan to the deities of earth, or to the souls to be loved, or to . . . spirits of the mountains, forests, rivers, and gardens." It symbolizes here "our sense of admiration of *veritas*," said Dr. Anesaki. "May it . . . serve as a link of affection and gratitude binding us to Harvard forever."

There followed then a stirring tribute to Harvard from non-Harvard men, delivered by Dr. Stephen Duggan, Professor of Political Science at the College of the City of New York and Director of the Institute of International Education. After addressing his audience, he turned from the speaker's lectern in the Tercentenary tribune to hand President Conant a letter "together with a check for five thousand dollars and a list of those who have joined in this greeting." No individual subscription to that gift was permitted to exceed fifty dollars; and "we whose names are subscribed to this message," said Dr. Duggan in behalf of his fellow contributors, "may assume to speak not only for ourselves but for a vast number of men and women who, like ourselves, have been reminded by this celebration of the incalculable services which our colleges and universities render to our civilization."

THE JAPANESE STONE LANTERN — "OF NEARLY THE SAME
AGE AS HARVARD, PERHAPS A LITTLE YOUNGER"

DR. ELLIOTT C. CUTLER, '09, RETIRING PRESIDENT OF THE
ASSOCIATED HARVARD CLUBS, PRESENTING THE PRESIDENT'S
CUP TO HIS SUCCESSOR, MACKEY WELLS, '08

More music: "Tercentenaria" by the Harvard band; clouds lowering in the sky; the great weather vane idle and unprophetic. And then John Harvard came a step nearer the present when Dr. Cutler introduced Dr. Thomas S. Hele, Master of Emmanuel College, Cambridge, and Delegate from our Mother University: "But in the University of Cambridge we do not only remember John Harvard, John Cotton, Thomas Hooker and those other thirty Emmanuel men, but we remember also Dunster of Magdelene, Eliot of Jesus, Norton of Peterhouse, Chauncy and Winthrop of Trinity, and we do not forget the men from Oxford. . . ."

Dr. Cutler announced the election of officers of the Associated Harvard Clubs for the year 1936–1937: Mackey Wells, '08, the new President,[1] received from him the President's Cup. The band played "Fair Harvard," which the audience sang, and the first of the great meetings of the Celebration was over.

There followed a luncheon in Memorial Hall given by the several Faculties in honor of the Delegates; a buffet luncheon for the Associated Harvard Clubs in the Memorial Hall Delta Pavilion; luncheon for ladies, in Sever Quadrangle; for alumni, in various rooms of Hollis, Stoughton, and Holworthy — headquarters, as at Commencement, of returning classes; luncheon in the Houses for Undergraduate Delegates. A single but important ceremony: dedication of the new Eliot Gate on Quincy Street (north of the Dudley Gate and opening on the grounds of the President's house). A gift of the Class of 1908, John

[1] Secretary, Nathan Pereles, Jr.,'04; Treasurer, Clarence B. Randall,'12.

Richardson, '08, made the presentation. This gate completes the final link in the iron fence which encloses the Yard. On one side of it is cut

IN MEMORY OF

CHARLES WILLIAM ELIOT

1834–1926

GIVEN BY THE CLASS OF 1908

On the other side, the final lines in the Henry James biography of the Olympian:

HE OPENED PATHS FOR OUR CHILDRENS FEET TO FOLLOW
SOMETHING OF HIM WILL BE A PART OF US FOR EVER

At 4 P.M. the second Symphony Concert was given in Sanders Theatre. The series concluded [1] in Symphony Hall on Friday evening at 9 P.M., when the orchestra was assisted by a Harvard and Radcliffe Chorus.

Evening: celebration continues: (*Salvete omnes!*). A dinner was given by the Council of Radcliffe College in honor of the Delegates of the Colleges for Women. The Harvard Chapter of Phi Beta Kappa held in Sanders Theatre its held-over meeting from Commencement week: Professor Bronislaw Malinowski, Delegate from the London School of Economics and Political Science and recipient of the degree of

[1] President Conant's last official Tercentenary word was uttered toward the close of this concert, when he went to the stage and said to Dr. Koussevitzky: "You and the members of the orchestra have given so much pleasure to the guests of Harvard during the past three days, that I venture to intrude at this point . . . to say just two words: 'Thank you.'"

Doctor of Science on the following day, was the orator. Associate Professor Robert Hillyer, '17, read the poem. From 9 to 11 P.M. in the Isabella Stewart Gardner Museum in Boston the Trustees of the Museum gave a reception in honor of the University and its guests, the Delegates from other Universities, Colleges, and Learned Societies.

But the public of Greater Boston will remember Thursday for the nine o'clock display of fireworks and illumination of the Charles River. A phantom census, which has never failed to supply the newspapers with accurate figures of parade and demonstration attendance, said that "350,000 people jammed their way into positions on both sides of the Charles between the Anderson and Weeks bridges as well as on the bridges." In the memory of one spectator this seems for once a wilful tabloid understatement: 3,500,000 is more nearly correct. But whatever the number, alumni and the public got the University's money's worth. Under clearing skies, rain seemed a thing remote. The cosmic scene-shifters were doing their best. But for us? . . . *In cœlo quies.* . . . Be that as it may, they were quiet enough until one of two barges starting from the West Boston bridge in the wake of secular tugs suddenly shot them with fire in a mighty brilliance of bursting stars and miniature comets. For two hours, at an acceleration of from two to six a minute, mine after mine was twice exploded — once on the powder barge and then in the local stratosphere. The second barge bore on its prow a plaster cast of John

Harvard and was trimmed with Japanese lanterns. Members of the Harvard band were also on board, but the honors for sound lay heavily on the side of the aerial bombs. Noise and light continued terrific. Flooded by thick color of red fire along its banks, the river shone like the crater of some equatorial volcano. It was Harvard's show for the public who could not attend the alumni festival. The Friday newspapers waxed rhapsodic: "The earth seemed to shake . . . after the deafening bursts of the bombs; and green, gold, and orange streaked the blackness, poised for a moment high in the sky . . . then floated slowly downward to fall hissing into the many colored waters." . . . "Continual cheers from a crowd whose size was almost as impressive as the scene." . . . "Not the arrival of the President, not the climactic finale when President Conant makes his speech . . . can touch this scene tonight for almost incredible pictorial beauty." So much for the press and for the fact.

The fireworks ended with a *Veritas* set piece — more modest, we may be surprised to discover, than the display at the 250th Celebration when in Jarvis Field there was "a representation of the statue of John Harvard, *standing in the midst of a gorgeous temple.*" And like that festival, the 1936 show was capped by a torchlight parade which passed singing and cheering up Boylston Street to the Yard, to the real statue (cheers), to the President's House (more cheers), and to a pop concert and dance in Memorial. *In cœlo quies* — and the chance of rain.

THURSDAY NIGHT: "OUT OF YOUR LIGHT, HARVARD!"

V

The weather forecast[1] for Friday, September 18, was issued Thursday evening by the Blue Hill Meteorological Observatory as "cool and overcast, no rain." (Sighs of relief.) In the Friday morning papers (late city edition) the tone had become more pessimistic: "Cloudy today, followed by rain tonight and tomorrow." No one cared about "tomorrow." Some 200 Tercentenary Aids and Marshals went to their windows early, fingered silk hats and

[1] RAIN CHECK: A post-Tercentenary letter to Jerome D. Greene from Charles F. Brooks, Professor of Meteorology and Director of the Blue Hill Observatory, records an exciting weather drama, and shows how carefully the meteorological factor was considered in deciding to hold the Friday morning exercises as originally scheduled: "*For* rain, was the inexorable and increasing rate of advance of the hurricane, centered Friday morning close to the Virginia Capes and moving northward. *Against* rain, was the steady high pressure here, the high and rising pressure and dry air on Mt. Washington, and the well-known tendency of morning sunshine to weaken cyclonic rainfalls. I have never known a more difficult problem in weather forecasting, nor, while successful, seen an important forecast come so close — a matter of only a quarter of an hour — to failure. You saw how it poured just after the end of the procession got into Widener! The rainfall of the storm, practically ending at 3 the next morning, was 3.40 inches in Cambridge and 5.78 inches at Blue Hill (B. H. was closer to the center)."

The specific forecast for Friday morning was given over the telephone to President Conant (9.37 A.M., E.D.S. time) by Salvatore Pagliuca, Chief Observer at Blue Hill: "Rain will be light and intermittent until 12 noon. Increasing thereafter. Less than 0.1 inch (probably 0.05 to 0.06 inch rain in Cambridge by 12 noon). No downpour before noon." President Conant asked if this could be "guaranteed." Mr. Pagliuca said that it could.

The Blue Hill verification record justifies that guarantee: "Intermittent light showers began at 8.03 A.M., E.D.S. time, at Blue Hill, giving a total of 0.08 inch rainfall by 12.30 P.M. (0.05 inch by 1.00 P.M. in Cambridge)."

looked out: Very doubtful. By 8.30, when most of them were arriving at University Hall to receive their red and silver batons, a few drops were actually falling. It fell intermittently during the early forenoon, but not hard enough by 9.30 o'clock to call for a rain programme. It may be, as Donne says, that

We are scarce our fathers' shadows cast at noon,

but it shall not be said of that ineluctable morning that any son of Harvard was afraid of the elements.

In what is always designated as the *old* Yard the alumni procession began to form at 9.30. Bugles blew then for Assembly; for "Ready" at 9.40; for "March" at 9.45. Charles Francis Adams, '88, was Chief Marshal of the Day; Joseph R. Hamlen, '04, Deputy Chief Marshal; G. Peabody Gardner, Jr., '10, Chief Aid; and Henry C. Clark, '11, Chief Flag Marshal. Flags for all living College Classes and for the Graduate Schools had been placed in advance in their designated sockets round the complete inner quadrangle bounded by Holworthy, University, Grays, and Massachusetts Halls. The Governing Boards, Delegates, Distinguished Guests, and Professors and Associate Professors of the University, assembled in Widener Library; all other officers of Instruction and Administration, between Thayer Hall and the Memorial Church. Undergraduates formed their procession in Sever Quadrangle. Outside in the Square, the umbrella business throve. All areas about the Yard were policed and kept clear of cars. Harvard families, guests and friends of the University, began thronging the theatre, spreading newspapers on the wet chairs, opening and closing umbrellas, settling themselves with the greatest fortitude and cheerfulness, by a few minutes past nine. The gates were crowded with arrivals for over an hour.

In the old Yard graduates old [1] and young formed in fours behind their flags, chatting with each other; optimistic, patient, wet. "The manhood and offices they brought hither today seemed masks; underneath we were still boys." It drizzled in spells. Those who had raincoats had two companions under them. Over in the theatre reporters and movie operators climbed to their simian retreats. Telegraph boys ran in and out with copy. Somewhere in the crowd the President's secret service men from Washington mixed themselves into the assembly. Streamers and gonfalons hung motionless and held fast to their primary colors. The outlook for the possibility of rain had changed to an outlook for the possibility of cessation. And from time to time there were lulls — readjusted collars, reshaken hats, and reorganization of self against September weather.

The parade started, not many minutes late, with a lift of flags and jovial, undampened spirit. The band played, feet stamped, collars were buttoned tighter, handkerchiefs appeared; men talked again like undergraduates as the moving classes passed the

[1] Of the youngest we do not know the names; but the names of two elders we know and record: Henry Munroe Rogers, '62, oldest living graduate of the College; and John Torrey Morse, Jr., '60, sole survivor of the oldest living College Class. In the procession these men marched directly behind the Chief and Deputy Chief Marshals.

waiting. It seemed to take endless minutes circling the old Yard to enter by the Tercentenary gate past the battery of relentless lens and unreeling film and into the swarming humanity gathered for the climax. But once in, things moved fast enough; for while the last and youngest classes were still finding seats and the audience rose and clambered upright on its chairs straining for a view, the doors of Widener opened and the academic procession began to descend the steps. An anxiously awaited moment! Down they came in twos, headed by President Lowell and President Conant, moving in measure through the parted Cambridge sea and the Marshals in a double wall of flags, to proceed directly to their places on the stage — behind the tribune and to the right and left. Rain fell upon them in gusty release. Dignitaries, Delegates, Judges, Ministers, Officers, Faculty. "Like moving day in the ark," as some wag has put it since; but exciting-solemn on that day, and wonderful alike for academic color and for the crowd in "veneration of their visible images," as Pater said. Such living drama was utterly new to the majority, who had not seen the earlier pageant in the Delta. It seemed new even to those who had. Down they went. We saw them ascend the stage. Under the pillars of the Church they settled finally like a flock of iridescent birds.

The wet weather had also turned cold. In the front rows, after stacking their flags in two flower-like clusters bordering the tribune, the Marshals retired under the smaller and less reliable trees. Rain

FRIDAY MORNING: MARSHALS DEPOSITING THE CLASS FLAGS

SEATS OF THE MIGHTY: PRESIDENT ROOSEVELT APPLAUDS. SITTING BESIDE HIM, LEFT TO RIGHT: VICE-CHANCELLOR LINDSAY OF OXFORD, PROFESSOR CARTAN OF PARIS, PRESIDENT LOWELL, AND BISHOP LAWRENCE. SECOND ROW AISLE, RIGHT, IS JEROME D. GREENE, '96

fell into silk hats during prayer, or was shaken from the leaves whenever a breeze came up. As the end of the academic procession arrived on the platform and the audience rustled into a prelude of repose, the alert observed that Franklin D. Roosevelt, '04, President of the United States, had slipped in from the back to his seat, front center. Others remarked the fact, and then the audience was on its feet in first applause. It was the Boston *Herald*, referring to this moment, which reported that "the rain spattered upon him with as much abandon as if he were a Republican." And "the world scholars," said the Boston *Globe* . . . "must have been impressed . . . by the informality with which the President of the United States took a seat and sat through the exercises . . . as though he were just one more of the many distinguished men upon the platform."

The University Marshal rose to make some magical prediction, and immediately the air was filled with a peal of bells transmitted across the Atlantic from the Tower of Southwark Cathedral. In a generation all but impossible to astonish, few of those assembled can have escaped some feeling of awe that this singularly moving circumstance could be. For a few minutes the bells rang in honest glory of sound: two worlds as one, John Harvard's land brought home. One listened, but humbly. When at last they faded out, and the Sheriff of Middlesex bright in blue uniform pounded his sword-in-scabbard three times and commanded traditionally: "The Meeting *will* be in order!" — the Meeting *was* in order; and the breach

between us and our own American past which we
had come to celebrate mysteriously healed.

On the platform, final courtesies were extended:
umbrellas offered and refused. Three Presidents sat
but a few feet apart declining all such protection;
though for a time (on photographic evidence) Mr.
Lowell shared the umbrella of Bishop Lawrence. A
mushroom growth of Jonas Hanway's unimproved
invention sprang up all over that acreage of listeners;
most of these umbrellas were black, leaving color to
the stage alone. . . . "*Salvete . . . vos certe feminae
ornatissimae et venustissimae (quarum pulchritudo
pluviae causa umbraculis nunc nimis operta est)*.". . .
The rain went on steadily about its business.

Dean Willard L. Sperry, Chairman of the Board of
Preachers, pronounced the Invocation. As the bells
had drifted in, his words floated off through the tribunal microphone, repeated in two hemispheres. An
uncanny business, used to it as one was: Word of
John Harvard's God, not now from England to his
wilderness, but from his wilderness to England. Following the Invocation the Pope Professor of Latin,
E. K. Rand, '94, delivered in Latin the Salutatory
Oration.

"*SALVETE OMNES!* Praeses magnifice, cum
coetu Sociorum et Inspectorum Universitatis Harvar-
dianae, patriae nostrae Praeses illustrissime cum Sum-
morum Conciliorum legatis praeclarissimis, gen-
tium nobis amicissimarum legati primarii, patriae et
civitatum et urbium magistratus huiusque civitatis
et legati et supreme dux, venerabiles quoque ec-

clesiarum pastores, accipite vobis debitam salutationem. . . .

"Nunc salutemus etiam mortuos illos immortales qui a parvo collegio condito ad universitatem instauratam magnam doctrinae urbanae et bonae vitae principia velut cursores lampada tradiderunt. . . .

"His igitur ominibus corroborati, non superbo sed pio et humili animo Deum optimum maximum precemur ut hanc universitatem tantae hereditatis nobis commissae haud indignam in nova et meliora semper saecula producat."

Between speeches, the speechless on the platform shifted a little under the weather. Once Mr. Conant was observed to wring the water from the gold tassel of his mortar board (an act preserved in the Tercentenary film). Stoics all! It was only the speaker who experienced momentarily the drier blessing of tribunal escape. "We of the audience [said an editorial philosopher later in the *Harvard Alumni Bulletin*] . . . were drawn together by our shared sense of the nobility of the occasion, not less than by a feeling of pride in our relationship, however humble, to the Harvard family. The ties that united us were almost as tangible as the rain itself, which bound us even more closely, perhaps, than the sun could ever have done.

"We saw the rain beating gustily in so many venerably beautiful faces; we saw it pattering down on rank on rank of gray heads which we knew contained as precious an agglomeration of brains as the world has ever seen gathered in one spot; we saw it splashing and staining their blazing silks and ermine; and — even as we hitched our drab trousers and turned up undistinguished collars about our humble necks — we noted the truly aristocratic disdain with which the demigods on the platform met the dull fury of the heavens. A remarkable demonstration of the power of mind over wet clothes, felt we, and gloried in imitating their noble indifference; pleased, too, in memory of urchin days, at the sight of so many silk hats preparing to meet their makers."

Professor Morison, as the Tercentenary Historian, delivered an address, "The Founding of Harvard College," which concluded: "From the small college here planted '*in sylvestribus et incultis locis*,' on the verge of the Western Wilderness, Harvard University has grown, and higher education in the United States is largely derived. So we are gathered here to commemorate our founders and early benefactors; to thank God for the faith, overriding all prudent objections and practical difficulties, that sustained them through poverty and struggle, in so ambitious and so excellent an enterprise." The Tercentenary Chorus [1] sang Gabrieli's "*In Deo Salutari Meo*." His Excellency James M. Curley, Governor of Massachusetts, brought Greetings from the Commonwealth. There followed then a ceremonial tribute by President Conant to our three ancestral Universities: Paris, Oxford, and Cambridge. As the names of these Universities were spoken by him, the Chief Dele-

---

[1] At least one member, George W. Wheelwright, '90, had also sung (as a freshman) in the Anniversary Chorus of the 250th Celebration, 1886.

gate[1] of each arose and was escorted by an Aid to a position side by side in front of, and facing, the President. After receiving in turn from the University Marshal the engraved addresses to each University, President Conant delivered orally their several words and presented them to the three Delegates. It was a mediaeval ceremony, still strangely fresh in the minds of many of that audience.

John Masefield, Litt.D. (Hon.) '18, Poet Laureate of England, and a poet to behold, in slow and enchanting voice read his poem[2] composed for the occasion:

LINES ON THE TERCENTENARY OF HARVARD COLLEGE IN AMERICA

When Custom presses on the souls apart,
Who seek a God not worshipped by the herd,
Forth, to the wilderness, the chosen start
Content with ruin, having but the Word.

So these, abandoning the English scene,
As spirit's solitary surety bade,
Ventured the wrath where Christ had never been,
Facing both sea and savage unafraid.

And here, amidst what then was desolation,
Of marsh and forest, these prepared and sowed
The spiritual seed-corn of a Nation
For life to harvest, when the Summer shewed.

---

[1] Paris: Professor Cartan; Oxford: Vice-Chancellor Lindsay; Cambridge: Dr. Hele.

[2] Copyright, 1936, by John Masefield. All rights reserved.

They were three thousand miles from help of kind,
Supply of tool or skill, support of store;
Their help was certainty within the mind
That, where the danger lurked, God went before.

Yet, when the certainty obscured, when doubt
Staggered the courage and made dumb the call,
When all the chaos of the waste without
Glared at the tired spirit to appal,

Then, to those setters forth, in their despair,
The need was grim for any rallying place,
That might give comfort from God's being there,
Or, if not He, a brightness from His face.

Then they remembered quiet far away,
Quiet and piety and bells in chime,
Among old college dwellings, long gone grey,
Built by the love of learning of old time;

And knew, that as that city had inspired,
Moulded and helped themselves, so they should found
Such blessed seeking-place for truth desired,
There in that thoughtless waste beyond the bound.

So, from their common will, they planned to raise
A spiritual house, that should inure
The white youth and the red youth to God's praise,
That, so, should prosper and be ever sure.

There was a preacher in that little band,
JOHN HARVARD, son of one from Stratford town,
Who may have shaken William Shakespeare's hand;
He, in himself, has title to renown,

For, when he preached, his earnestness would pierce
Beyond the bounded tenement of sense,
Into that living love, forever fierce,
Whose glory makes our stammering eloquence.

And it was he, who, with his dying gift
Of books and money, set this noble vine,
With roots too deep for ignorance to shift,
Its boughs aloft, in light, with living wine.

There is no record of his form and face.
One praised his preaching; little more is known.
He cast the spirit seed-corn of a race,
And died at barely thirty, having sown.

Untimely, to an unrecorded grave,
The unlimned ruins of his body passed;
This living monument of what he gave
Stands builded here in triumph, to outlast.

It has outlasted every other seed
Flung by the men and women of his day,
This excellence, the harvest of his deed,
Being divine, shall never know decay.

His act has brought us here; his dead hand brings
These thousands in his honour and his praise.
Which of our many peopled planet's kings
After three hundred years so surely sways?

In admiration and devout consent
Of gratitude to him, our thousands come
From Asia's age, from this new continent,
From Europe's all, and from his English home.

Would that his human eyes, untimely dead,
Freed from that quiet where the generous are,
Might see this scene of living corn made bread,
This lamp of human hope become a star.

Again the bond with our beginning tightened a little; the spirit perhaps burned brighter. The Poet bowed and withdrew, and the clapping swept away. But even poetry could not entirely dissemble the blackened character of the sky, though for an hour and a half (now almost forgotten!) there was no rain at all.

The Tercentenary Chorus sang Bach's "Hymn of Praise," and President Conant ascended the tribune to deliver his oration on "The University Tradition in America — Yesterday and Tomorrow." Several times in its course he was interrupted by applause; once, so vigorous that for a minute or more, smiling and vainly protesting, he was unable to proceed. At the end he received an ovation. He began on a note of affirmation; and what he said there is quoted here in full:

"Such a gathering as this could come together only to commemorate an act of faith. This assembly honors a vision three centuries old and in so doing reaffirms an intent of perpetuating an ideal. A hundred years ago President Quincy, writing of the founding of Harvard, used these words: 'On recurring to the origin of this seminary, our first feelings impel us to wonder and admire.' From such admiration grew the celebration of the two hundredth anniversary; with no less reverential feeling the sons of Harvard have once again met here to mark the turn of another century.

"MULTA SANE TALIBUS DUCIBUS DEBEMUS. . . ;" E. K. RAND, '94, POPE PROFESSOR OF LATIN, CONCLUDING THE SALUTATORY ORATION AT THE FRIDAY MORNING EXERCISES

"QUIET AND PIETY AND BELLS IN CHIME:" THE POET LAUREATE, JOHN MASEFIELD, READING

"The passage of a hundred years has enabled us to see more clearly the events which occurred between 1636 and the granting of the charter to the President and Fellows in 1650. Thanks to the labors of the historians we are able to appreciate more fully than did Quincy the spirit of the founders and to understand more completely the significance of their bold plan. And with the increase in our knowledge comes a more than proportional increase in our admiration. As you have heard, the Puritans' ambition was none other than to transplant to an untamed forest the ancient university tradition. They would be satisfied with nothing short of duplicating here in New England at least one college of Cambridge University. Carried forward by the strong tide of Puritanism, the enterprise was at first blessed with almost miraculous success. The goal might well seem to be in sight when, within twenty years of the founding, Oxford and Cambridge (then in the hands of dissenters, to be sure) recognized the Harvard degree as equivalent to their own. But many changes in both the mother country and the Bay Colony were yet to come. The enthusiasm for education in a new land waned, and even the second President of Harvard complained of those who desired 'to pull down schools of learning, or which is all one to take away the oyl from the lamps, denying or withholding maintenance from them.' The acorn had been planted, the young tree was alive, but its growth was slow beyond the expectation of those who had brought the seed to a wild, new continent.

"In the middle of the last century, in 1867 to be exact, the head of one of the Oxford colleges, an eminent scholar and educational reformer, saw no evidence that the university tradition had ever taken root in the United States. 'America has no universities as we understand the term,' he wrote, 'the institutions so called being merely places for granting titular degrees.' Taken literally this harsh judgment is undoubtedly false, and yet I venture to think that it is not a gross exaggeration of the situation which then existed. The new spirit moving within the educational institutions of this country had not become evident to those outside the academic walls. Another decade was to pass before a university was opened in Baltimore, national in its scope, and proclaiming boldly that 'all departments of learning should be promoted . . . and that the glory of the University should rest upon the character of the teachers and scholars . . . and not upon their number nor upon the buildings constructed for their use.'

"We commemorate today the daring hope of a group of determined men — a hope the fulfillment of which was long delayed; delayed, indeed, until within the lifetime of many now present here this morning. With feelings of gratitude we turn back through three centuries to pay homage to the faith that could see no obstacles and to ideals which are indeed eternal. But the real past which we salute is but yesterday. Harvard, together with all the other universities in this country, stands just beyond the threshold of a new undertaking. It is towards the

future of our common enterprise that on this occasion
we must direct our gaze.

"The future of the university tradition in America
— that is the problem that must concern all of us
who are assembled here today. But what is this tradition; indeed, what is a university? Like any living
thing, an academic institution is comprehensible
only in terms of its history. For well on a thousand
years there have been universities in the western
world. During the Middle Ages the air they breathed
was permeated with the doctrines of a universal
church; since the Reformation in Protestant countries these have undergone a slow and varied meta-
morphosis. But the essence of the university tradition has remained constant. From the first foundations to the present, four main streams have watered
the soil on which the universities have flourished.
These ultimate sources of strength are: first, the cultivation of learning for its own sake; secondly, the
general educational stream of the liberal arts; thirdly,
the educational stream that makes possible the pro-
fessions; and, lastly, the never-failing river of student
life carrying all the power that comes from the gre-
garious impulses of human beings. All four streams
are easily discerned bringing life to the English universities in the first half of the seventeenth century.
For this reason Oxford and Cambridge flourished;
and because they flourished, their sons who migrated
to this strange land desired to cultivate the same
sturdy tradition even in a wilderness.

"The plans of President Dunster and his collaborators reveal clearly what the university tradition meant to the Anglo-Saxon world of the seventeenth century. Harvard's founders insisted on the 'collegiate way of living,' thus recognizing the importance of student life. They knew the educational values which arise from the daily intercourse between individual students and between student and tutor. Their concept of professional training was, to be sure, largely cast in terms of the ministry, but they envisaged also training in the law and medicine. The liberal arts educational tradition they transplanted *in toto* from the colleges which they had left behind. And finally, their zeal for the cultivation of learning is made evident by the reference in the charter of 1650 to 'the aduancement of all good literature, artes and Sciences. . . .'

"Such, it seems to me, was the properly balanced plan of a university in a time when universities were flourishing; such, it seems to me, must be the idea of a university if institutions of higher learning are to fulfill their proper function in the times that are to come. But there have been periods of sickness, even of decay, in the history of almost every academic foundation. If one of the four vital streams I have mentioned either fails or swells to a torrent, thus destroying the proper balance of nourishment, then the true university tradition may perish. The cultivation of learning alone produces not a university but a research institute; the sole concern with the student life produces an academic country club or merely a football team manœuvering under a collegiate banner. On such abnormalities we need not dwell, but I should like to take a few moments to consider the disastrous effects of an overemphasis of either the liberal arts educational tradition or the element of professional training. This is a real danger at all times. For a university nourished exclusively from either one of these two educational streams always seems to the uninformed to be most healthy because they believe it to be most useful.

"Let us consider, first, the situation created when the proper balance is upset by disproportionate concern with general education. In this case the stream of learning and research inevitably dries up; indeed, some have contended that it should. Newman defined his idea of a university as 'a place of teaching universal knowledge, for the diffusion and extension of knowledge rather than the advancement.' In his famous essay he recommended 'a division of intellectual labor between learned academies and universities.' (In twentieth century terminology we should substitute the words 'research institute' for 'academy.') He believed that 'to discover and to teach are two distinct functions.' Newman's proposal amounted to eliminating one of the four vital ingredients evident in the life of the universities during their healthy periods. Unconsciously he was reflecting the condition of the English universities as he knew them before 1850 when they were still suffering from the long sleep of the eighteenth century. His proposition was in reality but a concise description of a disease. A few years later a prominent member of his own University, recognizing the condition as pathological, expressed himself in the following words: 'The colleges [of Oxford and Cambridge] were in their origin endowments for the prolonged study of special and professional faculties by men of riper age. . . . This was the theory of the university in the Middle Ages and the design of the collegiate foundations in their origin. Time and circumstances have brought about a total change. The colleges no longer promote the researches of science, or direct professional study. . . . Elementary teaching of youths under twenty-two is now the only function performed by the university, and almost the only object of college endowments. Colleges were homes for the life-study of the highest and most abstruse parts of knowledge. They have become boarding schools in which the elements of the learned languages are taught to youths.' When we read this indictment penned before the completion of the nineteenth century reform of Oxford, we may well ask: If the intellectual division of labor which Newman advocated and which still finds proponents in our own time is to be desired, why were the English universities in so unsatisfactory a condition? The accidents of time had destroyed the ancient function of advancing knowledge, and yet the institutions did not flourish.

"As further evidence, listen to what the Royal Commission of inquiry into the condition of Oxford had to say on this subject in 1850: ' It is generally acknowledged that both Oxford and the country at

large suffer greatly from the absence of a body of
learned men devoting their lives to the cultivation
of science and the direction of academical education.
. . . The presence of men eminent in various departments of knowledge would impart a dignity and stability to the whole institution, far more effectual
against attacks from without than the utmost amount
of privilege and protection.' Attacks from without —
the phrase has a modern ring. Events proved that
the Commission of 1850 was correct in its statement;
the changes which they advocated restored the confidence of the nation in its two ancient institutions.
They could not foresee, however, the reluctance of
certain sections of public opinion to welcome the
restoration of the true university tradition. They
did not realize how willingly the public often follows
those who argue for a separation of teaching and research! No better illustration could be found than an
article in the London *Times* published in 1867. The
writer endorses the general view that 'the university
is mainly a place of education for young men just before they enter upon life and should confine its whole
administration to this practical aim.' (Please note
the word 'practical'!) 'We are confident,' the article
continues, 'that this view is the one from which
Englishmen in general regard the universities. It is
a growing subject of discontent among the public
that the tutors and professors of both Oxford and
Cambridge are becoming more and more absorbed
in their own scientific pursuits.' And these remarks
at the time when the two ancient universities were

undergoing that revolution which restored them to health and enabled them to take the position of intellectual leadership which they now enjoy! So shortsighted is often the popular reaction to matters of education. Would the English public today wish to turn back to the years when the professors and tutors rarely yielded, indeed, to the temptation to cultivate sound learning and pursue new knowledge?

"There is comparatively little danger, however, that in the years ahead there will be any effective movement to turn the universities of this country into boarding schools. The cause for apprehension seems to me to lie in a different quarter. Even the most idealistic of those who lead public opinion too often insist on examining educational institutions through the dull glasses of immediate utility. To be sure, the promotion of learning usually appears to be worth saving even when viewed through such an unfavorable medium. The most relentless reformers are at least partially convinced that at some time almost all research may be materially rewarding. There is, however, a growing demand for more and more professional training, and there is a tendency to stretch the word 'profession' until it comprises every vocation. The utilitarian demand for specialized vocational training and the practical man's contempt for useless knowledge go hand in hand. When such influences gain control, an institution of higher learning supplies training, not education, and the promotion of learning is degraded to a vehicle for providing material well-being. The liberal arts conception of a

"HE WHO ENTERS A UNIVERSITY WALKS ON HALLOWED
GROUND:" PRESIDENT CONANT DELIVERING HIS ORATION

"SUCH A GATHERING AS THIS COULD COME TOGETHER ONLY TO COMMEMORATE AN ACT OF FAITH"

general education disappears and with it the institution's most important contribution to the land. The universities of a country are the sanctuaries of the inner life of the nation. When they cease to be concerned with things of the spirit, they cease to fulfill their most important function.

"If I am correct, then, in my interpretation of academic history, the future of the university tradition in America depends on keeping a proper balance between the four essential ingredients — the advancement of learning, the liberal arts college, professional training, and a healthy student life. None must be neglected; no one must be allowed to predominate unduly. If this balance can be maintained, the universities of this country, privately endowed and publicly supported alike, will function both as instruments of higher education and as centers for developing a national culture worthy of this rich and powerful land.

"Are we capable of evolving an American civilization commensurate with our opportunities? Surely this is the challenging question of the day. This is the question which transcends in importance even the most pressing demands of our troubled post-war period. Less than a century ago many people expressed grave doubts whether learning could be cultivated in a democracy. The last fifty years have proved them to be wrong. We can be proud of what has been accomplished in this republic, but only a start has been made. We must press on with all the earnestness and faith of those early settlers whose brave aspirations we honor by our ceremonies today.

"A wave of anti-intellectualism is passing round the world. We see evidences of it on every hand, but it is no new phenomenon. Before Harvard was founded, Bacon referred to the 'objections concerning the dignity of learning which arise from ignorance, appearing sometimes in the zeal and jealousy of divines; sometimes in the severity and arrogancy of politicians; sometimes in the errors and imperfections of learned men themselves.' With these sources of objections we are all familiar. But the anti-intellectualism of the present is in part a protest — a most ungrateful protest, to be sure, — against the benefactions of the learned world. It expresses a rebellion against the very triumphs of applied science, against the machines from which we would not be separated and yet towards which we feel a deep resentment. It is the expression of our weariness as we see an ever increasing wealth of new knowledge poured at our feet by the scholars of the arts and letters no less than by the scientists. Intellectual anarchy in our schools and colleges has been more or less rife for the better part of a hundred years. 'Will it never end?' we are tempted to cry in despair.

"To bring order out of an educational chaos is the mission of the liberal arts curriculum of our universities — that is why it is important that this ancient tradition be not overwhelmed. Those of us who have faith in human reason believe that in the next hundred years we can build an educational basis for a

unified, coherent culture suited to a democratic country in a scientific age, no chauvinistic dogma, but a
true national culture fully cognizant of the international character of learning. In this undertaking
the schools are involved quite as much as the universities, but the latter must lead the way. The older
educational discipline, whether we like it or not, was
disrupted before any of us were born. It was based
on the study of the classics and mathematics; it provided a common background which steadied the
thinking of all educated men. We cannot bring back
this system if we would, but we must find its modern
equivalent. Like our ancestors we must study the
past, for 'he who is ignorant of what occurred before
he was born is always a child.' In my opinion it is
primarily the past development of our modern era
which we must study, and study most exhaustively
and critically. We must examine the immediate
origins of our political, economic, and cultural life
and then work backwards. We must not, however,
spread the inquiry over so wide a range that the
average man will obtain only a superficial knowledge.
It does not seem to me to be a step in the right direction to dip our children first in one barrel of tinted
whitewash and then in another. The equivalent of
the old classical discipline is not to be found in a bow-
ing acquaintance with universal history and general
science, and an exposure to scattered examples of
art and literature. Our present educational practice
which insists on the thorough study of at least one
discipline is certainly sound.

"For the development of a national culture based on a study of the past, one condition is essential. This is absolute freedom of discussion, absolutely unmolested inquiry. We must have a spirit of tolerance which allows the expression of all opinions however heretical they may appear. Since the seventeenth century this has been achieved in the realm of religion. It is no longer possible for some bigoted Protestant to object if any person within the universities or without expounds sympathetically the philosophy of St. Thomas Aquinas. It is no longer possible for a member of the Roman Catholic Church to take offense at a critical discussion of Galileo's trial. Statements believed to be erroneous are met openly and fairly by counter arguments. But there is no persecution; there has been an end to religious bigotry in this country, and there are no signs of its return.

"Will the same conditions prevail in the future when political and economic problems are examined? Unfortunately there are ominous signs that a new form of bigotry may arise. This is most serious, for we cannot develop the unifying educational forces we so sorely need unless all matters may be openly discussed. The origin of the Constitution, for example, the functioning of the three branches of the Federal Government, the forces of modern capitalism, must be dissected as fearlessly as the geologist examines the origin of the rocks. On this point there can be no compromise; we are either afraid of heresy or we are not. If we are afraid, there will be no adequate discussion of the genesis of our national life; the door will be shut to the development of a culture which will satisfy our needs.

"Harvard was founded by dissenters. Before two generations had passed there was a general dissent from the first dissent. Heresy has long been in the air. We are proud of the freedom which has made this possible even when we most dislike some particular form of heresy we may encounter.

"In a debate in the House of Commons, Gladstone reviewed the history of Oxford and spoke of the lamentable condition of that institution during the reign of Queen Mary. Quoting an historian of that period, he continued: 'The cause of the failure is easy to discover. The Universities had everything, except the most necessary element of all — Freedom: which, by the immutable laws of nature, is always an indispensable condition of real and permanent prosperity in the higher intellectual cultivation and its organs.' With this conclusion all who cherish our heritage must agree: without freedom the prosperity most important for this country cannot be achieved — the prosperity of our cultural life.

"The university tradition in this country has been sustained through three centuries by the courage and sacrifice of many men. An ever-increasing number of benefactors have followed John Harvard's example. Patrons of learning have not only favored Harvard with their gifts but have established and aided other universities throughout the nation. In cities and states, institutions have been founded and supported from the public funds. In all our colleges learned men have labored with little material reward to 'advance learning and perpetuate it to posterity.' Teachers of the young have so lived their lives that the coming generations might be inspired with a love of wisdom. All this devotion on the part of those concerned with higher education stands as a clear witness to the significance of what was here envisaged three hundred years ago. He who enters a university walks on hallowed ground.

"If we attempt to sum up in one phrase the aim of higher education, we can do no better than to speak of 'the search for the truth.' A little more than a hundred years ago when President Quincy was exploring the Harvard archives, he came upon the early record book in which is the famous drawing of the Harvard seal as specified by a vote of the Overseers in 1643 — the open books with the word *Veritas*. Delighted by his discovery Quincy restored *Veritas* to the college arms, but it was not until 1885 that this word found a permanent place upon our seal. To me there is an arresting symbolism in this bit of apparently accidental history. It is significant that the Puritan founders chose the word *Veritas*, for this word is the touchstone of the real university tradition. And it is fitting that the original seal was finally re-adopted just when Harvard was developing into a great modern University.

"When the Puritans wrote *Veritas* upon the open books, they had in mind two paths by which truth could be obtained: one, Revelation as interpreted with the aid of human reason; the other, the advancement of knowledge and learning. Bacon expressed the spirit of the age which was to follow when he declared that a man cannot 'search too far or be too well studied in the book of God's word, or in the book of God's work, but rather let men endeavor an endless progress or proficience in both.' In the present century a French mathematician wrote, 'The search for truth should be the goal of our activities; it is the sole end worthy of them. . . . If we wish more and more to free man from material cares, it is that he may be able to employ the liberty obtained in the study and contemplation of truth. . . . When I speak of truth,' he continued, 'I refer to scientific truth but also moral truth of which what we call justice is only one aspect. . . . Whosoever loves the one can not help loving the other.' This same thought was expressed by President Eliot in an address in 1891 which stands as a challenge to our time. Speaking of a university as a 'society of learned men,' he defined their goal as 'the incessant, quiet, single-minded search after new truth, the condition for both the material and intellectual progress of the nation and the race.' The intellectual progress of the race — during the coming century of academic history what gifts will the American people bring to further this great advance? A hundred years from today the record will be read. With humility but with hope we look forward to that moment. May it then be manifest to all that the universities of this country have led the way to new light, and may the nation give thanks that Harvard was founded."

Music again by the excellent chorus under Professor A. T. Davison: Händel's "Let Their Celestial Concerts All Unite." And following this, the impressively brilliant spectacle of the conferring of sixty-two honorary degrees. Forethought once more lent mechanical precision to an aesthetic end. What might have lasted long never seemed to drag. President Conant read each citation, handed the diploma (which had been handed to him) to one of four active Aids who conveyed it to the recipient. The Delegate so honored rose from his seat in a flash of color, received it, and sat down amid applause. Sixty-two men:[1] the pick of the world's most learned, recognized elsewhere and before, but here gathered as one body representing nearly all the important fields under the Arts and Sciences, for the sole purpose of honoring Harvard and receiving in turn her highest pronouncement of merit. As the list was read, and man after man of different race and nation, thought and training, bowed response, the layman leaned obviously to names like Jung and Eddington; and yet seemed no less cordial in applauding the scholar of whose reputation he was probably politely ignorant.

The list is too long for this account, but a few of President Conant's citations in the tradition of Commencement may be quoted in illustration:

EDWARD JOSEPH DENT: Doctor of Music. A professor of Cambridge University famed for his historical studies of

[1] None of these men had previously held any Harvard degree.

THE CONFERRING OF SIXTY-TWO HONORARY DEGREES: PROFESSOR JOHN HAROLD CLAPHAM OF THE
UNIVERSITY OF CAMBRIDGE RECEIVING HIS DIPLOMA FROM AN AID

that melodious art which is the common heritage of all western nations.

SIR ARTHUR STANLEY EDDINGTON: Doctor of Science. A student of the cosmos who peers within the atom and surveys the expanding universe, an expounder to the multitude of the poetry of modern science.

WESLEY CLAIR MITCHELL: Doctor of Letters. An American economist whose influence has extended far, noted for his study of the business cycles which, despite all efforts, still revolve.

LEOPOLD WENGER: Doctor of Laws. A lawyer deeply versed in the origins of his profession, a man of learning profound in his knowledge of the legal systems of antiquity.

WERNER WILHELM JAEGER: Doctor of Letters. A critical student of that great master who once dominated the universities, an eminent teacher of the eternal wisdom of Aristotle.

HU SHIH: Doctor of Letters. A Chinese philosopher and historian, the inheritor of the mature wisdom of an old civilization who guides with courage and understanding the spirit of a new age.

CHARLES GUSTAV JUNG: Doctor of Science. A philosopher who has examined the unconscious mind, a mental physician whose wisdom and understanding have brought relief to many in distress.

KARL LANDSTEINER: Doctor of Science. The master of the science of immunology, the discoverer of those fundamental principles which made blood transfusion possible, saving countless lives.

MICHAEL IVANOVICH ROSTOVTZEFF: Doctor of Letters. The social and economic historian of the Roman Empire, whose fruitful study of antiquity accumulates for all who read centuries of rich experience.

ETIENNE GILSON: Doctor of Letters. An expounder to these chaotic days of the serene and ordered philosophy of the Middle Ages, that great synthesis of faith and reason.

The audience sang properly "O God, Our Help in Ages Past" (Isaac Watts), and after Benediction by Bishop William Lawrence, '71, the Meeting concluded — now in a downpour which lasted the rest of the day. One happy corollary not well understood is that Dignitaries, Delegates, and other guests were ushered immediately back to Widener where the Corporation's Ganymede had provided what the *Bulletin* in thin disguise called "comforting nectar." But not to know, of course, was not to envy.

The principal one o'clock luncheons that day were the Chief Marshal's to the Governing Boards and their Guests (Memorial Hall), and that of the Harvard Alumni Association (Memorial Hall Delta Pavilion). Those farthest in kept the driest. It was obvious even then that the Meeting of the Alumni Association scheduled for the Tercentenary Theatre that afternoon would have to be held in Sanders. To lose, at the last minute, the open-air advantage of vividness and size seemed hard. But with apparently no effort the right switches were thrown, the right mechanical changes made, the right notice given, the public address system plugged in for the Memorial Church, Memorial Hall, the New Lecture Hall, Music Building, Jefferson Physical Laboratory, and the Continental and Commander Hotels (by broadcast), where the now divided congress of the morning might convene. As with everything else, the afternoon exercises were also released on the air. One could stay at home and listen.

Sanders Theatre will accommodate some 1,200 people. By two-thirty it was practically filled with an audience admitted only by ticket, and composed largely of Officials, Dignitaries, Delegates, and University guests. Officials and Dignitaries crowded the stage. Such an intimate gathering, after one so vast, bore even closer to the heart of things. President Lowell presiding carried most of us back to another administration. When all tests for the broadcast were completed and the doors locked safely Symphony fashion, the familiar figure rose and went to the lectern. Did a strange thing seem to happen? One almost fancied that he held back for a second as if indrawn by some old reluctance. But "the Greek agility" of his mind, as Professor Morison has called it, must have persuaded him even as he persuaded at once his seen and unseen audience. With the freshening memory of what had transpired that day and for many days before, it was impossible to see and hear him now and remain unmoved. He began in what familiar style! shaking his head characteristically in emphasis:

"As wave after wave rolls landward from the ocean, breaks and fades away sighing down the shingle of the beach, so the generations of men follow one another, sometimes quietly, sometimes, after a storm, with noisy turbulence. But, whether we think upon the monotony or the violence in human history, two things are always new — youth and the quest for knowledge, and with these a university is concerned. So long as its interest in them is keen it can never grow old, though it count its age by centuries. The means it uses may vary with the times, but forever the end remains the same; and while some principles, based on man's nature, must endure, others, essential perhaps for the present, are doomed to pass away.

"Education is as old as man; and many of the arts of life were learned and taught long before any historic record. All the domestic animals we use today were tamed no one knows how long ago; the planting of seed goes back to a past invisibly remote; so do many of the modes of preserving food; and each of these advances must have been carefully taught to children, or they would have perished with their inventor. Teaching cannot be less ancient than the oldest art that ever was transmitted; and with the growth of knowledge it has become more and more important for the public welfare; yet we now know less about it with certainty than of many other arts of later origin.

"The inevitable breakdown of the ancient fixed curriculum, coupled with larger openings for enjoyment, on one side, and on another the vast expansion of knowledge, have raised two of the serious questions of our time. The first has made it hard to impress upon youth the value of scholarship. Apart from a definite, visible application that value has seemed to them difficult to measure — pale as compared with athletic and social achievement. Its significance for the man himself, for the development and attitude of his mind appears so vague, the fact that all real attainment comes by personal effort, — a process of self-education under guidance so contrary to his ideas of how teachers should labor and students absorb, — that it is not easy to make him see these truths.

"Some years ago a class orator [1] remarked that only as they near graduation do students learn what the real object of college is, and this seemed very unfortunate until we reflect that when they do know it they are educated men. With the problem of inciting scholarly ambition all institutions of higher learning have been wrestling; happily by different means, for there is no single formula for solving it, and all experiments, if judged by their results, are good.

"The vast increase of knowledge has raised obstacles of a different kind for the professors, and for all others bent on contributing to learning. The first result was a division of the field of thought into self-contained sections under separate departments; but that has proved defective because there are no natural barriers to knowledge. It has overflowed and undermined the fences, rushing as a flood across them, and hence the later effort has been to bring the various laboratories, the whole contents of the libraries and the professors themselves into as close contact as possible, so that every man may draw whatever he needs from the great supply.

[1] Edward C. Aswell, '26.

"A university is, indeed, a thing that moves and grows. In deepest gratitude to its progenitors we recall on this occasion that three hundred years ago Harvard College was born, a brave babe, with only one teacher — the President himself — who at first gave all the instruction, and possessed all the learning, it contained. Now it is one of the great universities of the world; one of the reservoirs and springs of knowledge that, beginning in the Middle Ages, have developed into what they are today.

"The vast learning stored on the shelves of the libraries, and in the minds of all the scholars, in a great university no single man can compass; of the channels leading to new knowledge, one can explore but a small part. The treasures are well-nigh inexhaustible, the opportunities limitless; and open not to the members of the institution alone, but almost for the asking to anyone who has the desire and the capacity to use them. From our forebears, who in less propitious times have taught and labored and hoped here, we have inherited a priceless trust which will be fostered until, as the Arabs say, the stars grow old, the sun grows cold, and the leaves of the judgment book unfold.

"The generation that have now retired, hoping in their own time to have made their contribution, have passed the torch that burns here to you, President Conant, and your colleagues, to bear farther and higher on the way."

Mr. Lowell then introduced President Conant whose remarks rested largely on Harvard's plans for

UNIVERSITAS CANTABRIGIENSIS

UNIVERSITATI HARVARDIANAE

SALUTEM

INTER EXULES, qui olim fidei causa novam terram ultra terminos Atlanticos petiverunt, legimus fuisse Cantabrigienses sexaginta; quorum in honorem, cum Academiam fundarent patres, Almae Matris memores mutaverunt appellationem Oppidi Novi ut semper litteras scientias religionem Cantabrigiae nomen revocaret. Illud etiam memoria dignum videtur quod nondum in Nova Anglia septem annos fuerant antequam collegium desiderabant; ita flagrabant et scientiae et religionis amore. Hoc enim praecipue se timere confessi sunt, ne mysteria Dei tractaret clerus litterarum expers. Spem quoque alebant non solum tutandi sed et promovendi doctrinam quam posteris relinquerent.

Quam spem, ut memoria vetera et recentia repetimus, non vanam fuisse videmus. Scilicet ut apud poetam Latinum legimus promisisse Apollinem

  Ambiguam Salamina nova tellure futuram,

—quod nomen Graecis magnam gloriam significabat,—agnoscimus et nos, non invidi sed gratulantes, ambiguam iam esse Cantabrigiam, nec sine terrae additamento nominandam, ne fiat confusio, dulcissimus quidem error, immo et documentum quanta gloria floruerit Academia prima Novae Angliae.

Nil ergo amplius possumus vobis precari quam ut Fortuna, quae tria iam saecula vobis faverit, semper arrideat.

Dabamus Cantabrigiae
*anno Salutis nostrae mcmxxxvi
die quinto decimo mensis Maii*

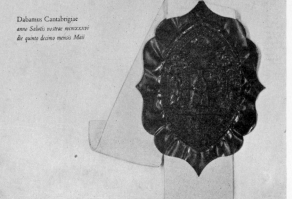

MATERNAL GREETINGS FROM THE UNIVERSITY OF
CAMBRIDGE

the future and on the Tercentenary Gifts already received.

Mr. Lowell rose again and spoke for perhaps six minutes, glancing once or twice at his watch. It is not likely that many were aware of the identity of the next speaker until his name was pronounced. As though he were in the same room and had himself risen from a seat on the platform, The Right Honourable Stanley Baldwin, Chancellor of the University of Cambridge and Prime Minister of England, responded as Mr. Lowell ceased. His message, for the second time in the celebration, united miraculously the new world and the old. Precise as that electric appointment, his message carried clear:

"As Chancellor of the University of Cambridge it is with special pride that I send greetings to Harvard University on the occasion of its Tercentenary. The Cambridge men from the beginning identified themselves with Harvard; and graduates from Trinity, Emmanuel, and Kings were on the first governing body three hundred years ago.

"Above all, it was an Emmanuel man, John Harvard, who supplied the funds for the outward and visible sign of the new College and his admirably chosen library for its inward and spiritual grace.

"Nor can I forget that it was a graduate of Harvard — his father and grandfather were Cambridge men — who gave his name to Downing Street [1] in which I live.

[1] Sir George Downing, Bart., M.P., Class of 1642.

"May God's providence, which has watched over Harvard since its first home had to be fenced in to keep out the wolves, continue to bless it, adorned as it now is with magnificent buildings and celebrated throughout the world as a great center of learning.

"May Harvard men remain faithful to the great traditions of liberty which are the common glory and heritage of all the English-speaking people of the world, and may we all, as university men, though we cannot hope for the special fame that is John Harvard's, aspire to be remembered in our time in the moving words applied to him by a contemporary:

"'The man was a scholar and pious in his life, and endeared to the country in life and death.'"

When he had finished speaking, Mr. Lowell replied:

"If a university can have one mother, Cambridge is our mother; for Harvard was founded mainly by her graduates. Six years after landing on these shores our forefathers set up a college, and named the town after the place where they were trained. The University of Cambridge fostered our early days by granting to our degrees equality with her own. From her we have drawn inspiration and example — not least in these latter times. To her sons we owe a vast debt in science and in letters. In the light she has shed we have rejoiced.

"If she be the mother of Harvard, she is, through Harvard, the ancestress of most of the universities and colleges in the United States. It is right that we should turn to her in gratitude this day; and, now when we have prospered, should seek her approbation.

"Therefore, in behalf of the thousands of Harvard graduates here assembled, I thank you for the kind words you have said in bringing to us, on this our three hundredth birthday, the greetings of our parent University."

Following the singing of the Seventy-Eighth Psalm, and a speech by Judge Learned Hand, '93, President of the Harvard Alumni Association, Mr. Lowell came forward. "The next speaker it would be impertinent for me to introduce to you, or to any American audience. He is the fourth graduate of Harvard College to hold the office of Chief Magistrate in our nation — two of them named Adams, and two Roosevelt. Gentlemen, The President of the United States!" The audience rose in great applause. President Roosevelt:

"I am here today in a joint and several capacity. First, as the President of the United States. Second, as Chairman of the United States Harvard Tercentenary Commission, which is composed of five members of the Senate, five members of the House of Representatives, a representative of the United States Army and one of the Navy, and two representatives of the universities of the United States, the distinguished Presidents of the Universities of California and North Carolina. Finally, I am here as a son of Harvard who gladly returns to the spot where men have sought truth for three hundred years.

"The roots of Harvard are deep in the past. It is pleasant to remember today that this meeting is being held in pursuance of an adjournment expressly taken one hundred years ago on motion of Josiah Quincy.

"At that time many of the alumni of Harvard were sorely troubled concerning the state of the nation. Andrew Jackson was President. On the two hundred and fiftieth anniversary of the founding of Harvard College, alumni again were sorely troubled. Grover Cleveland was President. Now, on the three hundredth anniversary, I am President.

"In the words of Euripides:

> There be many shapes of mystery.
> And many things God makes to be,
> Past hope or fear.
> And the end men looked for cometh not,
> And a path is there where no man sought.
> So hath it fallen here.

"In spite of fears, Harvard and the nation of which it is a part have marched steadily to new and successful achievements, changing their formations and their strategy to meet new conditions; but marching always under the old banner of freedom.

"In the olden days of New England, it was Increase Mather who told the students of Harvard that they were 'pledged to the word of no particular master,' that they should 'above all find a friend in truth.'

"That became the creed of Harvard. Behind the tumult and the shouting it is still the creed of Harvard.

"In this day of modern witchburning, when freedom of thought has been exiled from many lands which were once its home, it is the part of Harvard and America to stand for the freedom of the human mind and to carry the torch of truth.

"The truth is great and will prevail. For centuries that grand old saying has been a rock of support for persecuted men.

"But it depends on men's tolerance, self-restraint, and devotion to freedom, not only for themselves but also for others, whether the truth will prevail through free research, free discussion, and the free intercourse of civilized men, or will prevail only after suppression and suffering — when none cares whether it prevails or not.

"Love of liberty and freedom of thought is a most admirable attribute of Harvard. But it is not an exclusive possession of Harvard or of any other university in America. Love of liberty and freedom of thought are as profound in the homes, on the farms, and in the factories of this country as in any university.

"Liberty is the air Americans breathe. Our government is based on the belief that a people can be both strong and free, that civilized men need no restraint but that imposed by themselves against abuse of freedom. Nevertheless, it is the peculiar task of Harvard and every other university and college in this country to foster and maintain not only freedom within its own walls but also tolerance, self-restraint, fair dealing, and devotion to the truth throughout America.

"Many students who have come to Harvard in the

past have left it with inquiring and open minds, ready to render service to the nation. They have been given much and from them much has been expected. They have rendered great service.

"It is, I am confident, of the inner essence of Harvard that its sons have fully participated in each great drama of our nation's history. They have met the challenge of the event; they have seen in the challenge opportunity to fulfill the end the university exists to serve. As the Chief Executive of the nation I bring you the felicitation of our people. In the name of the American nation I venture to ask you to cherish its traditions and to fulfill its highest opportunities.

"The nation needs from Harvard today men like Charles William Eliot, William James, and Justice Holmes, who made their minds swords in the service of American freedom.

"They served America with courage, wisdom, and human understanding. They were without hatred, malice, or selfishness. They were civilized gentlemen.

"The past of Harvard has been deeply distinguished. This University will never fail to produce its due proportion of those judged successful by the common standard of success. Of such the world has need. But to produce that type is not, I am sure, the ultimate justification that you would make for Harvard. Rather do we here search for the atmosphere in which men are produced who have either the rare quality of vision or the ability to appreciate the significance of vision when it appears.

OBVERSE AND REVERSE OF THE TERCENTENARY MEDALLION,
DESIGNED AND EXECUTED BY GRAHAM CAREY, '14

(Actual size)

"Where there is vision, there is tolerance; and where there is tolerance, there is peace. And I beg you to think of tolerance and peace not as indifferent and neutral virtues but as active and positive principles.

"I am not, you will observe, conceiving of the university as a mere spectator of the great national and international drama in which all of us, despite ourselves, are involved. Here are to be trained not lawyers and doctors merely, not teachers and businessmen merely; here is to be trained in the fullest sense — man.

"Harvard should train men to be citizens in that high Athenian sense which compels a man to live his life unceasingly aware that its civic significance is its most abiding, and that the rich individual diversity of the truly civilized State is born only of the wisdom to choose ways to achieve which do not hurt one's neighbors.

"I am asking the sons of Harvard to dedicate themselves not only to the perpetuation but also to the enlargement of that spirit; to pay ardent reverence to the past but to recognize no less the direction of the future; to understand philosophies we do not accept and hopes we find it difficult to share; to account the service of mankind the highest ambition a man can follow, and to know that there is no calling so humble that it cannot be instinct with that ambition; never to be indifferent to what may affect our neighbor; always, as Coleridge said, to put truth in the first place and not in the second; these, I would affirm, are the qualities by which the 'real' is distinguished from the 'nominal' scholar.

"It is only when we have attained this philosophy that we can 'above all find a friend in truth.' When America is dedicated to that end by the common will of all her citizens, then America can accomplish her highest ideals. To the measure that Harvard participates in that dedication, Harvard will be justified of her effort, her purpose, and her success in the fourth century of her life."

"The Shores of Harvard," by M. A. De Wolfe Howe, '87 (music by Holst), previously a part of the Commencement service, was sung by the Tercentenary Chorus. Mr. Lowell then introduced James Rowland Angell, President of Yale University.

"Despite my possession of two Harvard degrees [said Mr. Angell], it is with no little astonishment that, as a simple Vermont Yankee representing conservative Connecticut orthodoxy, I contemplate my temerity in appearing here — *in partibus infidelium*, as it were. It may be a case of fools rushing in where angels should fear to tread. In any case, it is with peculiar pride and gratification that Harvard's eldest daughter, her nearest of kin, is permitted upon this festal occasion to join with all the learned world in singing her praises and in wishing her yet many centuries of invaluable service to mankind. One cannot possibly add anything to this chorus of acclaim, couched in most felicitous phrase, with which for days these halls have been ringing.

"Founded, and in her early years largely guided, by men of Harvard lineage, Yale has always felt herself bound by ties of special intimacy to the parent institution — albeit cherishing at times toward Harvard sentiments of more than doubtful moral elevation, sentiments almost always warmly reciprocated by Harvard. It is not without reason that each speaks of the other as its dearest enemy. But today Yale comes bearing only the olive branch and a garland of bay leaves.

"I cannot quite repress the temptation to pause and pay a purely personal tribute to a group of great Harvard men to whom I shall always stand indebted. I came here as a young man in the early '90's to study under William James, Josiah Royce, and George Herbert Palmer. These brilliant scholars left on my mind an indelible impress, and, together with John Dewey, then at Michigan, gave me the essential *Weltanschauung* with which I have gone through life. I command no words which will adequately convey my obligation to them.

"I have also enjoyed most delightful relations with three eminent Presidents of Harvard. Charles William Eliot offered me my first academic job and at a time when I much needed it. When I came to preside over Yale, President Lowell greeted me in the most generous and cordial manner. During his administration no suspicion of tension between Harvard and Yale ever arose which he and I in frank conference could not quickly banish. Yale could ask no more sincere friend than he. For President Conant, in the few years I have had the pleasure of knowing him, I have come to entertain the most genuine admiration and a very warm regard. In his great address this morning the sturdy and vigorous qualities of his mind and character were in striking evidence. Incidentally I may say that, as I was drawing about me my bedraggled robes at the close of the ceremonies, I overheard one of your distinguished graduates,[1] who was exhibiting a condition of complete saturation, remark: 'This is evidently Conant's method of soaking the rich.' I naturally feel a purely academic interest in the fate of the Harvard rich, but I want to put in a plea for your indigent country cousins, whose endurance is fast approaching its limit. But let me turn back from these more personal matters.

"No one can view the history of universities without being profoundly impressed by their amazing vitality and longevity. Nations come and go, dynasties rise and fall, civilization itself is radically transformed, but the great universities live on. Clearly they minister to enduring needs which men will not allow to go unsatisfied; and Harvard, for all her relative youth on the roster of the world's great seats of learning, — and even in the western world three exceed her in age — has abundantly exemplified some of the noblest of the traits to which the university as an institution owes its preservation. Familiar as they are, we can hardly too often remind ourselves of them, nor too firmly fix our resolution upon their protection.

[1] Laurence McKinney, '12.

"With unflinching courage Harvard has steadfastly fought for complete intellectual liberty. The struggle has been sometimes with religious bigotry, sometimes with political usurpation, sometimes with social prejudice, and each of these forces can exercise tremendous pressure upon institutions dependent for their existence on public approval. But despite occasional set-backs, she has always ultimately won through, so that freedom of thought and speech within her halls has ever been safeguarded for scholars. Again she has been catholic in cultivating a constantly widening range of intellectual interests. Starting as a Puritan college with half a dozen subjects of study, she has persistently broadened her reach until now there is no appreciable territory in the empire of the mind which is alien to her. This achievement has often required something of the daring of the pioneer, a willingness to venture exploration and conquest in new lands whose value no one could confidently predict. It has always meant defiance of the smug conservative wedded to the idols of the past. But all of these accomplishments would have been shadowed by mediocrity had she not so resolutely sought for her faculties men of the very highest intellectual calibre. It is at this point after all that the truly matchless values of a university are to be found, values which can only be fully exploited by the choicest youth of each generation.

"Incident to the execution of her ends she has assembled one of the world's most magnificent libraries, where are preserved the imperishable treasures of the human spirit manifest throughout the ages, and has supplied to her scholars all the technical facilities which superb laboratories and exhaustive collections afford. For all these achievements and many more that must here go unnumbered the world owes Harvard a lasting debt of gratitude, and especially are the colleges and universities of America, and whosoever loves learning and books, debtor to her.

"In the somewhat fatuous and futile comparisons of institutions with one another, so dear to the heart of certain rather literal and metallic-minded folk, she is often put first, and judged by many criteria she doubtless deserves such a rating; but her essential human significance is not thus to be measured. Rather does it reside in those sterling qualities which are indigenous to her, reflected again and again in her history: vision and imagination tempered by wisdom, high moral courage and candor, unswerving allegiance to intellectual liberty with unquestioning reliance upon integrity of thought, unshakable belief in the ultimate worth of sheer intelligence and in the incomparable value of the great mind. These are some of the most obvious traits which have brought her undying fame and won for her three centuries of noble history in which every patriotic citizen must take pride.

"Would that we could turn away from this feast of felicitation with no feeling but one of joy in a great achievement and placid confidence in what the future holds in store for Harvard and for all other universi-

ties. But to do so would argue us completely oblivi-
ous to certain of the most tragic happenings of our
time. I have no appetite for playing the part of
Banquo's ghost, but there is another picture of the
learned world, unhappily all too true, which ought
not wholly to escape us and for a brief mention of
which I beg your indulgence.

"In three of the great nations of the world the university as the home of intellectual freedom, of truth
for truth's sake, is essentially extinct. Some of the
most revered seats of learning have overnight been
transformed into propaganda factories. How much
further the process may go no one can foresee, much
less predict. But almost in the twinkling of an eye
one great set of values for which generations of men
had struggled and sacrificed, and to which men paid
the tribute of deep and sincere reverence, have been
wiped out. 'It can never happen here,' say the self-
complacent — and let us hope that they speak truly.
But already there are current among us movements
hardly less ruinous, if they go unchecked, than those
which on the Continent have despoiled ancient universities of their most precious birthright.

"Perhaps most often in our own educational history it has been the attack of sectarian bigotry which
our colleges have had to resist. Harvard history re-
veals not a few such episodes. But today the most
menacing attack comes, as it has repeatedly in the
past, from the political side. In one form it is precipi-
tated by allegedly patriotic organizations committed
to maintain in schools and colleges their own particu-

lar conception of loyalty. The motives of these mis-
guided folk are, I doubt not, often excellent. But
they have opened the cover of Pandora's box and we
may well be fearful of the issue. For example, in
many schools American history may now be taught
only in terms these self-appointed patriots deem
desirable. Teachers who will not prostitute their
knowledge and convictions to the often ignorant bias
of these worthies must find other jobs. Sometimes the
results desired are sought through the imposition of
teachers' oaths. Sometimes by more direct methods,
but the outcome is always the same, i.e., the assign-
ment to busy-bodies, often moronic in mentality, of
the power to terrorize able and honest teachers, with
the ultimate ruin of the morale of the teaching force.
Few teachers would object to taking a loyalty oath if
other citizens did the same, especially editors, priests,
preachers, radio speakers, playwrights and actors,
and the directors of movies, all of whom exercise a far
more direct and potentially corrosive influence on
public opinion. But as now applied, the oaths inevitably reflect upon the character of the teaching
profession. Moreover, their sponsors can hardly hope
thus to accomplish their real purpose, for supposing
that rarest of animals, a disloyal teacher, no oath is
going to prevent his making his real views felt.

"In this connection I wish I could share the belief
expressed by President Conant this morning that we
have little or nothing more to fear from religious
bigotry. But I cannot wholly forget the Ku Klux
and the Black Legion of Detroit and the Scopes trial

CAMBRIDGE SKY: THE FLOODED TOWERS OF ELIOT AND LOWELL IN EVENING LIGHT ALONG THE CHARLES

and the fact that in several states it is against the law to teach the doctrine of evolution.

"Pernicious and dangerous as are these trends in their ultimate possibilities for simple honesty and truth in education, the attack through taxation is far more immediately serious. This assault takes two general forms: — one, the attempt of local governments to impose real estate and other taxes upon endowed institutions which are tax exempt by legislative enactment. The merits of this issue are far too complicated to canvass at this time. Suffice it to say that most communities now making these efforts originally offered bonuses of one sort or another to attract the institution in question away from other communities which desired it, and furthermore, that the presence of the institution results in the expenditure of very large sums of money in the community which otherwise would go elsewhere. These considerations wholly disregard the moral and intellectual values of a college to a community upon which President Eliot chiefly based his brilliant and convincing presentation of Harvard's case to the legislature of Massachusetts not so many years ago. The frequency with which this effort to tax is repeated all over the country, the number of cases which have come before the courts (in all of which up to this time, so far as I know, the courts have sustained the contention of the colleges) is disturbing, for it reflects a trend in public sentiment which, if it grow, may prove irresistible. Some colleges might in time adjust themselves to the situation were local taxes levied, but the immediate effect upon many institutions would be substantial bankruptcy and destruction.

"President Conant's encouraging report on Tercentenary gifts to Harvard makes such anxieties seem rather groundless here. Apparently Harvard men have not heard of the depression, but your poor relations are faced with quite a different situation.

"The second threat to endowed institutions from taxation arises from the relentless impositions on income and on legacies of benevolent individuals, two sources from which the endowed institutions have in the past secured a large part of their essential resources. This tendency unhappily coincides with a period of marked reduction in interest rates, with a resulting decline in the normal income of these institutions — and even college professors cannot live on air, although their critics often imply that hot air is their chief diet. Men high in authority have been of late quoted as intimating that taxation would shortly be so used as to compel all endowed colleges and universities to come under state or federal control.

"Now I am myself a product of the public high school and the state university, for both of which I cherish the most profound gratitude and respect. I only regret that I do not represent them more worthily. But I say with the most solemn conviction that to strangle the endowed educational institutions, or to convert them into mere creatures of the state, would be to destroy supreme and irreplaceable values into whose creation centuries of the most devoted and unselfish human effort have been poured. It would be a tragedy different in kind from, but comparable in character with, the ruin of the great universities abroad. That crying human need must be relieved, and that drastic taxation is an incident to such a process, I fully realize. But I bespeak the thoughtful and sympathetic consideration by this great alumni body of the unavoidable repercussions upon endowed education which inevitably flow from certain types of taxation now increasingly in vogue. We may be spared the sacrilege visited upon many of our sister universities in Europe, but let us not be blind to the grave and imminent dangers which already confront us at home.

"To fair and stately Harvard her devoted sons offer their most profound and affectionate homage. May the Almighty continue to shed upon her the light of His favor that in all the centuries to come she be ever found marching on to new victories of the spirit with the torch of truth held high in her blessed hand."

Following President Angell, Alexander Dunlop Lindsay, Vice-Chancellor of Oxford University and Master of Balliol, spoke briefly in gracious tribute to Harvard and her place in "this strange Utopian flower, this free commonwealth of universities all over the world." The chorus sang "*Laudate Dominum*" (music by Frederick S. Converse, '93); and after George Russell Agassiz, '84, President of the Board of Overseers, had made his address, President Conant called on Jerome D. Greene to stand up: "The name of one man who will be forever connected with this Anniversary, the man whose loving care has been reflected in every detail." Long and affectionate cheers; and then the meeting was prophetically adjourned, after the example of 1836, to the year 2036. President Lowell, as Chairman, called on President Conant for the motion. President Conant made the motion, adding a word of explanation: "Yesterday morning we connected the present with the past; this afternoon we look toward the future. . . . One of the undergraduate speakers referred to Josiah Quincy, Jr.'s prophecy [1] that 'a century will soon roll away, and there will be another clan-gathering of the sons of Harvard. They will come rushing, as it were, on the wings of the wind, from every quarter of our land.'

"Gentlemen, I repeat Quincy's prophecy and venture to extend it by changing one simple word: 'On the wings of the wind' from every quarter of the globe will throng the Alumni of this University when America celebrates the beginning of the fifth century of higher education.

"Mr. President [to President Lowell], I move that this assembly of the Alumni be adjourned to meet at this place on the eighteenth of September, 2036."

Mr. Lowell said:

"Before putting the motion I want to say a word in its favor. If I have read history aright, human institutions have rarely been killed while they are alive. They commit suicide or die from lack of vigor, and

[1] Bicentennial, 1836.

then the adversary comes and buries them. So long as an institution conduces to human welfare, so long as a university gives to youth strong, active methods of life, so long as its scholarship does not degenerate into pedantry, nothing can prevent it from going on to greater prosperity. In spite of the condition of many things in the world, I have confidence in the future. Those of you, therefore, who believe that the world will exist one hundred years hence, and that universities will then be faithful to their great purpose, will say 'Aye'; contrary-minded, 'No.' "

It was a unanimous vote.

The Meeting was adjourned.

The assembly sang "Fair Harvard," and with that the Tercentenary Celebration was formally closed.

VI

By that adjournment the sense of conclusion was not complete. It was certain only that the mediaeval color had disappeared. The alumni population of Cambridge and Boston suddenly fell to normal; in a week or ten days the College would open the 301st academic year. Something was over, and something was about to begin. But it was not certain that the festival which we had shared, to which so many had lent their fellowship, had not clarified the future equally in clarifying the past. If this were so, the ennobling spirit of those three days must remain with us long after the events shall have been forgotten. Perhaps now — like the Puri Indians — for yesterday, today, and tomorrow we have only one word. We have looked back and found new strength; shall we look forward and keep it?

The consideration of "this homespun past of ours" at any time, during any celebration, can only be a good and cleansing thing. Lowell recommended it fifty years ago — "to remind ourselves how poor our fathers were, and that we celebrate them because for themselves and their children they chose wisdom and understanding and the things that are of God rather than any other riches." We have considered it again, in all humility and in fortifying company. Harvard is still her own proof "that there is true ascension in our love." We may take that phrase from Emerson, who was one of us.

When Harvard celebrated in 1936, the Alumni did not gather alone. We shall remember with pride that there were others and greater to do her honor. Nor did we for our part (let us hope) merely fumble with sentiment. The many alertly persuading elements of costume, companions, voice, and music absorbed our attention, but significance cut deeper than sight or sound. Something of that final week is still unadjourned; something of that meeting will continue independently, and in strange and far-off places. And so long as such is the fact, we may start the count of another hundred years and evoke in the name of courage what was really our ancestors' worth.